ELK HUNTING SECRETS

239 Tips and Tactics

from members of the
Rocky Mountain Elk Foundation

THE LYONS PRESS
Guilford, Connecticut
An imprint of The Globe Pequot Press

Copyright © 1999 by The Globe Pequot Press
Previously published by Falcon Publishing, Inc.
First Lyons Press edition, 2006

The Lyons Press is an imprint of The Globe Pequot Press.

10   9   8   7   6   5

Illustrations by Wm. Gamradt

ISBN 1-56044-938-1

Library of Congress Cataloging-in-Publication Data is available
on file.

Printed in Canada

CONTENTS

It pays to do your homework, using maps
and binoculars—plus a few techniques you
probably never considered—to locate elk
before the hunt begins.

Once you know where the elk are, you need
to get close. Easier said than done. But more
easily done if you know these tricks.

Elk have us backed clean off the map when it
comes to sense of smell. But you can make up
for your handicap by adding to your store of
knowledge and gear.

Whether you're trying to find an animal, or
trying to find your way, these ideas can help
you stay the course.

From the sometimes conflicting advice on the
best rifles and cartridges for elk, you can still
gather information to help decide what's best
for you. Whatever rifle you choose, you'll find
pointers here on how to make the best use of it.

FOREWORD

The Rocky Mountain Elk Foundation proudly presents the most recent printing of *Elk Hunting Secrets*, first published in 1999, to offer advice and field-tested secrets to help improve the success of elk hunters.

The information and ideas shared in this book came from some of the best elk hunters in the world—Elk Foundation members. Within this humble but highly informative text, you will learn from experienced hunter-conservationists important tips and tricks, ranging from tracking skills, to how to choose rifles and cartridges, to the effectiveness of calls and calling. The passion for the hunt and the reverence we all share as hunter-conservationists for this magnificent quarry are reflected by all who contributed to this guide.

The Rocky Mountain Elk Foundation offers *Elk Hunting Secrets* with great pride and dedication to our 150,000 members and 11,000 active volunteers. Because of your support and commitment, we have protected and enhanced more that 4.2 million acres of habitat for elk and other wildlife in our 22 years as an organization.

As you read the vignettes contained in this fine book and think about the sage advice provided by your fellow members, please keep in mind that you are part of a wonderful tradition—you are the recipient of guidance handed down from one generation of successful hunters to the next. This book is part of our tradition and commitment to pass on to future generations our passion for elk hunting and our respect for wild places.

The Elk Foundation is committed to ethical hunting and respect for the individual animal and the land. We believe that honest hunting for free-ranging animals benefits the hunter, the animal, and our society.

Enjoy your copy of *Elk Hunting Secrets*, tuck it into your pack, and read it by campfire light in the wild country you helped protect. I wish you good luck in all of your hunting adventures. See you in elk country!

J. Dart
President and CEO, Rocky
Mountain Elk Foundation
Missoula, Montana
March 2006

INTRODUCTION

A hunter can always use another gun, another knife, another week of hunting season—and another tip on how to get an elk. A few years back some people around the Elk Foundation decided we could all use a whole book full of hunting tips, and after some solemn consideration decided that the best source of elk hunting expertise would be our own members and supporters. When we put out the call for tips from *Bugle* readers and RMEF website visitors in 1997, the response was terrific. By April of 1999 when we wrapped it up, we had a collection of over 300 field tested, woods proven, authentic ideas for better hunting from elk hunters all over the country.

There's something for everyone—from novice to expert—in this collection. A few of these tips will be familiar to most hunters, but no matter how long you've been hunting or how many books you've read, or what old timer showed you the ropes, you're going to find at least a few new tricks here.

You'll find tips that'll save you some grief, and maybe your life. Tips that'll give you an edge in locating elk, tips that'll help you get in close to the animal you're after, tips that will help you and your weapon perform to perfection when the moment of truth is at hand, and tips that'll give you an edge in getting the meat, hide and antlers home in good shape. You'll find ideas here that will surprise you, some that will make you laugh and shake your head (in spite of the fact that they may well work . . .), and some that will make you say "If only I'd known that years ago!" (Or last year!)

Surprisingly, we found very little outright duplication among the tips people sent us. While some came real close to saying the same thing, there was usually enough difference to warrant printing both, if only to honor the folks who were thoughtful and energetic enough to write up each tip and send it in. But there is at least some small, useful detail that distinguishes every tip in this book. There might be some good reason, for example, to use a balloon instead of scotch tape to keep rain out of your rifle barrel. Or electrician's tape instead of scotch tape. If nothing else, the different methods our contributors chose for keeping moisture out of their barrels—or out of their frizzens, nipples and pans—also point the way to innovation. If you don't happen to have any balloons or tape or fingernail polish with you, the variety of methods and materials described in this book may help you think of something else that might work in a pinch.

Whether you hunt with bow and arrow, black-powder or centerfire rifle, whether you hunt alone or with partners, afoot or with pack and riding stock, you'll find something to apply to your particular hunting situation, and help you hunt safely, efficiently and effectively. Looking back after your next successful hunt—reflecting on all the things you did right to bring down your elk and put good meat in your freezer and a trophy on your wall—you just might realize that a key factor in your success was something you picked up here.

Happy reading, and happy hunting.

Don Burgess
Bugle *Hunting Editor*

SCOUTING

It pays to do your homework, using maps,
binoculars—plus a few techniques you probably never
thought of—to locate elk before the hunt begins.

Unfortunately, I do not often have the advantage of
scouting an area before opening day, thus I depend
on my ability to read topographic maps to familiarize
myself with the area. United States Geological Survey
(USGS) maps or U.S. Forest Service (USFS) maps of
any hunting area can be purchased through local
sporting goods stores or by mail order. With these
maps, you should be able to identify natural features
important to game patterns such as north and south-
facing slopes, clearings and forested areas, drainages
and watering holes. You will also be able to identify
man-made features such as roads, buildings, mines
and railroad tracks. Information specific to your area
such as travel restrictions and protected areas are usually located on Forest Service maps. For convenience,
I carefully cut out sections of the maps where I will be
hunting and laminate them so that they will not get

damaged in the elements. This also prevents having to noisily fold and unfold maps when I am hunting.

Kyle Blasch
San Antonio, Texas

I can't say enough about pre-season scouting. If you don't get out there and look for them, your odds of success aren't too good. During summer months look for tracks around water. Elk like to bed down on high ridges. September is great for scouting. If you don't know where to start, drive to a place where you can see a lot of open hillsides about two hours before dark. Scan the slopes with binoculars. Be patient. Wait until it's too dark to see before you give up. Then try another spot the next time.

Richard Robinson
Washington, Utah

Pre-season scouting is very important in harvesting an animal consistently. Pre-season scouting can give clues to bedding and feeding areas, game trails and water holes. Patterning elk by thorough scouting will make for a more successful hunt.

Trevor Yochum
Lewiston, Idaho

Make time and take time to scout. It really pays to do your homework. When you find elk, stay at a far distance. Just watch them. Don't get so close to them that they notice you and spook. If they sense danger, they are probably going to change their feeding, traveling, and bedding areas and times, while you'll be trying to find which county they were last seen in.

Rick French
Wasilla, Alaska

Sometimes hunters, in an effort to locate game and sign, will step right on top of elk the day before the season opens. The elk panic and escape to maybe three canyons away. Then on opening day, they're gone and can't be found. If we find fresh sign in an area, we leave that area alone, because we know the elk are there.

Mark Cunningham
Crowley, Texas

Many people will come to an area three or four days prior to the season opening in order to "scout it out." I'll often speak to these folks after the season opens and they'll say something like, "When we got here, there were elk all over the place, and now we can't find any." Then they'll tell you how four or five of them literally walked every square yard of a several mile area without seeing any elk. Of course they aren't seeing any elk. They've scared every elk in the drainage somewhere else.

Do most of your scouting by use of a topo map prior to coming to hunt. Then spend your scouting times sitting and glassing likely looking areas and verifying whether it is good habitat. Don't walk through bedding and feeding areas, and for goodness sakes, don't practice your bugling techniques just to see if they work. I've even seen people bugling at elk from their vehicle! Every elk that figures out a call he responded to came from a human being is one less elk that can be called in during season.

If possible, when you arrive at your hunting area, spend a few days camping on the fringes, but not right in the middle of the best elk hunting. One area that my dad and I have consistently seen and shot elk at is occasionally ruined because someone drove to the end of the road and set up camp. What the people didn't know is that the little valley they camped in is a major route that the elk use on a daily basis to move from their feeding area to their bedding area several miles away. Obviously, since the camp is set up right in their path, they will adjust their routes to avoid human contact. The funny thing is, if the people would just camp a mile further down the mountain, they would have an equally good camping area, and see more game in the process.

Glen Trainor
Granby, Colorado

Most elk hunters have topo maps of the areas they frequently hunt. Those maps will become infinitely more valuable if you mark on them the locations you see elk or other game, or anytime you kill an elk or know of an elk killed. After a few years the same patch of dark timber or aspen stand will have more than its share of marks, and it will become apparent where the really good spots in your hunting area are.

Scott Campbell
Colorado Springs, Colorado

If you hunt from a tree stand, try to get out early to do your scouting, and then place your tree stand and do your limb clearing at least several weeks before the season starts. The less you bother your hunting area as the season approaches the better.

Jeff Keller
Bend, Oregon

The hardest part of elk hunting is finding the elk. Spend the first couple of days on high ridges glassing the area. Once elk are located, you can move into them the next morning or evening.

Todd Corsetti
Pocatello, Idaho

One of the best methods of spotting elk is glassing from a high vantage point late in the afternoon. If elk are spotted, they usually will be in the same general area next morning.

Jack Yates
Hazlehurst, Massachusetts

Prolonged and thorough glassing will increase your opportunities to kill game. When glassing opposing slopes for game, here's the technique which works best for me: First glass the areas within rifle range, then begin to thoroughly glass the facing slopes. I do this by glassing a line from the ridgeline straight down to the end of the line of vision. I then shift the field of view to the right (or left) slightly overlapping the line just covered, and glass a line back up to the ridgeline, and repeat this process till all the area in front of me has been carefully covered—then do it all over again, and again, and again!

Charles N. Pirtle
Las Cruces, New Mexico

Learn new areas where elk may be by using topo maps. Look for places elk will move from feeding and bedding. Try to hunt ridge tops for tracks.

Mike Mobbs
Olympia, Washington

Elk, when not bothered, will follow patterns of travel, particularly when coming to and going from feeding areas. When scouting a hunter should side-hill a drainage until finding game trails which are used for coming up or down to these feeding areas. Usually traversing the ground in a circular fashion will reveal such routes. Elk seldom travel horizontally at the same elevation.

Dick Taylor
Oregon City, Oregon

During one of my first elk hunts many years ago, a veteran elk hunter told me that no matter how cold I felt, it was a safe bet that the elk were hot. Look for them to be bedded on shady slopes, in deep canyons, and in the thickest part of the brush. On early season hunts, this is particularly true. Although your teeth are chattering, the elk are looking for relief from the heat.

Grady E. McCright
Las Cruces, New Mexico

While elk are heavy into the rut, the cows will tend to move to level ground where they can be bred easier. Elk do not usually breed on sidehills or steep inclines. This tip may help you find where the elk are hanging out in your area a little easier.

Barney Hammond
Calhan, Colorado

Pay close attention to trees scarred by elk. Learn to differentiate between bite marks and antler rubs. Rubs tend to have deeper scars or marks at the bottom of the rub area. Teeth, on the other hand, tend to leave wider impressions on the upper end of the bite area. Bite marks are obvious when they show where the two incisors scraped. Antler marks are a bit more random.

Read everything you can get a hold of on elk, elk hunting and elk habitat, and assess the area you hunt for applicability. Conditions vary from one location to the next and some techniques or information might not apply where you hunt. For example, some suggested hunting techniques may work much better in some areas than in others; or some types of forage may be found more palatable at different times of the year, depending on the area. Ultimately, you should use any information you can find to aid you in intimately learning and knowing the area(s) you hunt, and the elk that live there.

Carry a notepad and pencil with you whenever you are hiking, scouting or hunting. Take notes of all sign including feeding, bedding, tracks (direction traveling), rutting areas, etc. and note the location, time of year, weather and anything else that will help you recollect and piece together the elk puzzle in your hunting area.

Make a habit of taking a camera (one-time use cameras work well, and are lightweight) with you whenever you are hiking, scouting or hunting in your hunting area. When you get to a good vantage point, take photographs of the surrounding areas. These types of photos may be extremely valuable, especially when used in conjunction with a good topo map. You can learn more about your hunt area by studying photographs, along with good topo maps in the off-season (or back at camp), to help figure out possible hunting strategies.

Larry Burnett
West Jordan, Utah

Laminate topo maps and mark with special pens for noting animal sign. Transpose GPS coordinates onto topo maps to remember locations. Laminating also makes the topo maps last a lot longer.

Don Ramsden
Winona, Minnesota

A good way to locate elk is to spend some late evenings and nights bugling into canyons and valleys from the ridgetops or canyon bottoms. Once the elk

are located, you can move into the area the following morning.

Todd Corsetti
Pocatello, Idaho

Don't spend all of your evenings in camp. Elk that
are heavily hunted become even more nocturnal
than usual. I'll leave camp an hour or so after dark
and walk logging roads. I use a cow call, and elk
seem to answer more readily than in the daytime. If
you find them in the evening, you can usually find
them near the same place in the morning. If you
can't find them, it's unlikely they'll move into the
area during the daylight hours.

Andy Cates
Federal Way, Washington

One strategy that has helped me locate elk is to hike
very early in the morning in an area that is not hunted much by others. I walk from three to five miles in
the dark listening for the sounds of cows or calves. If
I hear elk I stop and wait until it gets light enough to
hunt. When hunting an area three to five miles from
my rig or camp, I sometimes hike back out in complete darkness. While I am doing this I am listening
for elk. If I hear some elk sounds, I will try to find
the same area in the morning darkness. This works
best if it is not windy. When it is quiet, elk sounds

carry quite a distance, especially if I am near timberline and the elk are above me. Knowing the trails
well from daytime hikes helps me to navigate in the
dark. I carry two small flashlights and use them spar-
ingly.

Gaylynn "Griz" Becker
Bismarck, North Dakota

Try setting your alarm clock for around midnight
and go for a stroll down the trail. I find many times
elk may not be vocal until sometime after dark and
may also stop being vocal just before daylight when
other hunters are snoozing. Also, you can begin
hunting a couple of hours before daylight. Leave in
the dark and get in on a vocal bull and then wait till
daybreak to make the final ambush. This way you
can get the jump on other hunters if hunting in a
popular area.

Reginald Brooks
Saskatoon, Saskatchewan

Aspen groves can be good places to search for elk.
Elk need nutritious and varied forage, water and
thick cover; aspens can provide cover and forage,
and water usually isn't too far away. Aspen groves,
generally found on south-facing slopes, can produce
as much as one ton of food per acre, which is about
10 times as much as many pine and spruce forests

Scouting

provide. The inner bark of aspen approaches grass hay in nutritional value. In many parts of the southwestern U.S., aspens are the single most important food source for elk.

Because fire rejuvenates grasses and forbs, areas recovering from recent forest fires are also great places to look for elk. Elk forage in a burned area can be 50 percent more nutritious than it was before the burn.

Mike Zimmermann
Houston, Texas

Scouting and preparing for the hunt is a year-round process. As you read various hunting books, watch hunting videos, peruse hunting articles and visit with other hunters, highlight those ideas, tips, notes, hotspots, etc., that relate to you and/or your area. Then, set up a disk on your computer to record the information, using a separate disk for each game animal. As hunting season approaches, print your tips and review. This will keep all those ideas fresh on your mind without having to read everything again.

Dan Blackwell
Canon City, Colorado

Elk hunting is something we need to think about every day, not just during a few weeks each fall. If you are not on a first name basis with the game warden and elk biologist of the area you hunt, then you are not doing your homework. Call your wildlife department today and ask how *your* elk are doing.

Tory Taylor
Dubois, Wyoming

Plan your hunt, but don't become too enamored with your plan. Elk are where you find them, and can change their location in a minute. When starting a new day or a new hunt, be alert to recently made tracks or even that wild elk odor. The top of the ridge that had seemed like the place to be during an evening planning session may not be productive the next day. Too many hunters become overly concerned with following a previously planned route. In doing so, they ignore sign and their own instincts. Stay flexible and go where the elk are.

Gerald Westesen
Bozeman, Montana

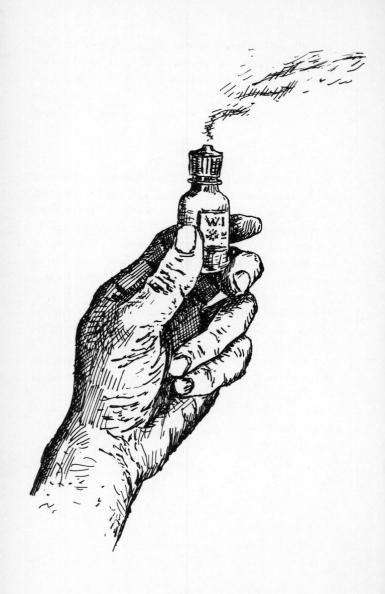

CLOSING IN

*Once you know where the elk are, you need to get close.
Easier said than done. But more easily done if you
know these tricks.*

One of my hunting tips for checking wind:
1. Purchase a small squeeze bottle.
2. Fill with cornstarch.

When you are looking for a squeeze bottle (i.e., parts store, dollar store, grocery store, etc.), try and find the smallest one you can. When you're in the field and want to know the wind direction just squeeze the bottle, and a plume of powder will come out and blow in the direction of the wind.

Leon Kerns
Boise, Idaho

I have talked with scores of experienced elk hunters and find that very few have actually heard an elk drumming. Biologists tell me that it is a result of the rutting bull beating his penis against his stomach. It sounds like a deep clunking sound. I like to describe it as similar to the sound of a log rolling around in a 55-gallon drum.

I have killed bulls on two occasions as a direct result of recognizing this sound. Last fall in British Columbia we bugled in a heavy non-typical bull. However, when he got within a hundred yards of us he shut up. I was fully camouflaged, hiding at the base of a small spruce tree, wondering where the bull had gone, when I recognized a faint drumming sound. I was looking in the direction of the last bugle. I slowly turned 90 degrees and could just make out the tip of his horns and his lower chest and front legs. He was hiding in the brush about 50 yards from me. This bull was not going to expose himself until he identified the bull that was bugling at him. I am absolutely certain that if I had not recognized the drumming this bull would have eluded me.

George McCoy
Girdwood, Alaska

If you are "in close" to a herd of elk and for some reason they spook, you can sometimes stay with them by running with them. You are just one more set of feet making noise running through the woods and sometimes they will not go very far before they stop to see what spooked them. Do not run with an arrow on the rest or a bullet in the chamber of a rifle, though. Use good judgment and be safe.

Jeff Keller
Bend, Oregon

I would recommend that hunters and photographers carry a cow call. Several times when I've encountered elk on the move, I've blown on my cow call and gotten them to stop long enough for me to get a good look at them.

Phil Trunkle
Billings, Montana

Where you are hunting and how you got there are secondary to good stalking skills. Practice being very still and very quiet. If God gives you a shot make it a good one. Once you can manage these few things you can move on to other disciplines. Otherwise, try not to disturb the natural environment.

Ross D. Keeling
Lawrence, Kansas

When you see an elk rump in the timber keep in mind that if you try to see its head, it will probably see you, too. Do not try to adjust yourself so that you see

Closing In

its head. Instead, if the elk is facing to your right, step to your left slowly and try to see more and more of its body. Once your vision has increased from its rump to its gut and now chest, if it's a bull you will likely see antlers above its chest or neck. If it's not the elk you want, it makes for entertainment. I have used this tactic successfully on several occasions.

Gaylynn "Griz" Becker
Bismarck, North Dakota

While archery hunting one evening, I viewed a herd from across the canyon. I observed the hesitancy of the herd bull to allow cows to cross a clearing into the trees—he was fixated on the trees. The next morning the herd was in the same location, so I decided to pursue. I stalked to within 200 yards—within the trees. I could smell the musk! Since I was fixated on the herd I completely ignored the possibility that there might be other elk in the area. I walked right up on a nice satellite bull who was bedded in a perfect spot to also watch the herd. Had I been alert to the signs, I would have realized that there was something in the trees, and been prepared. As it turned out I spooked the satellite bull before I could come to a draw. Moral: read all the signs and don't make foolish or short-sighted assumptions. The signs are often subtle, but nonetheless important.

Walter M. Eiker, Jr.
Landenberg, Pennsylvania

If you intend to shoot elk from your vehicle, plan on punching your tag every ten years. If you walk only hearing or sight distance from your vehicle to hunt elk, plan on putting an elk in your freezer every five years. If you walk to where the elk live, plan on dining on elk steaks every year.

Tory Taylor
Dubois, Wyoming

From the time a hunter loads his rifle to the time he unloads his rifle he should never set it down. Learn how to do things with one hand. Always be hunting. That moment of calm reflection, breathing the clean mountain air, enjoying the scenery or just relieving yourself must be done in the context of hunting.

George Gallagher
Woodstock, Illinois

To me hunting is patience, persistence, skill and luck! Probably in that order. After a cold hard day of hunting, it is sometimes difficult to stay put until the end of shooting time. On a December elk hunt in northern New Mexico, I once sat watching a big park for the last 2½ hours of shooting time, in a screaming icy wind. I saw six other hunters come along a trail along the far side of that park during the last 30 minutes of shooting light. My partner and I made a quick stalk on a bunch of elk that came into the park 10 minutes before the end of shooting time and killed a cow and bull. We were successful mainly due to persistence. Always try to stay in a likely spot until legal shooting time expires.

If you see elk feeding their way into the timber in the morning, but can't get into position to intercept, resist the temptation to go into the timber after them. Go hunt elsewhere, or do camp chores, and return about 3 P.M. and pick a vantage point with favorable wind currents, and it is likely that same bunch of elk will exit the timber very near to where they entered it that morning.

Always carry a book in your pack. You may luck into one of those hard-used elky areas that speak (and reek!) of elk. You may be too far from camp to leave and then later return to that spot—or you may simply choose to keep disturbance to a minimum by finding a vantage point (sheltered from the elements if necessary) and pleasantly spend several hours reading and observing nature, becoming an accepted part of the scenery, until that ol' bull ambles out and gives you that clean shot that we all dream of!

Charles N. Pirtle
Las Cruces, New Mexico

When walking game trails searching for bulls, use the two-man system. Space yourselves 35-40 yards apart and "cow talk" to one another, preferably with two different cow calls to enhance the authenticity of the scenario. Remember, no two cow elk are going to sound exactly alike. If there's a bull in the area, he could come in silent, so always be alert.

Jerry J. Farber
Saskatoon, Saskatchewan

If you have to cover a distance before still hunting, stay on game trails as opposed to the crackling dry leaves of the woods.

Butch Grusing
Fountain, Colorado

In any hunting area where they run cattle, I carry a cow bell on my pack and let it rattle as I walk. When I break a limb or kick loose a rock, I shake it to relax the elk. They are used to cow bells on lead cows and will not be as alert as when hearing an unexplained noise.

Ferrin "Griz" Dodson
Santa Clarita, California

I usually have one of my hunting partners take me as high as any road will allow and will walk my way back down to camp. This traverse from elevation allows me to look for sign that the elk have started adjusting to the season and environment. First I look for edible grass. When I find this, I may cut horizontally across the elevation and look for beds and shelter. Elk will travel to water, but are essentially grazing animals. Food and bed-down shelter always seem to be in close proximity, while water can be at the bottom of a draw or canyon. Once I find this, I plan my hunt along those elevations and so far have been fairly successful. This tactic is only good for the opening two or three days of the season, and after that I will sit and watch mornings and evenings and rely on other antsy hunters to walk around and spook the animals. I can't tell you how many times I have had hunters pass me and not see me because I was sitting still and just watching, blaze orange and all.

Bob Thompson
Fort Collins, Colorado

I do most of my hunting in the thick timber of southwestern Montana. Seems that elk love to bed for the day at or just below the crest of a knob, ridge or hill. This gives them several escape routes depending on where danger (hunters!) might approach from: over the top of the knob (and out of sight) if approached from below, right or left; around the knob (and out of sight) if approached from one side or another; or a speedy downhill sprint into the timber if approached from the top of the knob. So, when working through the trees, if you notice a contour change at a knob, hill or ridge, be even more cautious than usual, in order to get the drop on 'em. Or consider setting up an ambush there with more than one hunter.

Robb Larson
Bozeman, Montana

When still hunting or stalking, train yourself (and your eyes) to constantly scan the landscape all around you. Keep your head up while on the move. Don't look down any more than necessary (but don't forget to look for tracks, droppings, feeding areas, bedding areas, wallows, etc., on the ground, too!). It takes some practice to be able to walk noiselessly without constantly looking down. (It's a bit like fishing—you're unlikely to catch anything if your line isn't in the water!)

Larry Burnett
West Jordan, Utah

A simple way for checking the changing wind direction is to use any type of very fine, unscented natural powder, such as chalk or cornstarch. Put it into a small plastic squeeze bottle with a small hole in the top. Hold it at arm's length and squeeze it, and watch as the dust follows the wind current. Light-colored powder is more visible for dusk and dawn hunting. A small bottle lasts the whole season.

Alan C. Johnson
Rapid City, South Dakota

Tape a small (1-by-1½-inch) plastic zip-locked bag full of goose down to your gun or bow as an inexpensive but very effective way for testing wind direction and currents. Cut a small X in the side of the bag with a sharp knife or razor. The down will be contained unless you pull it a piece at a time through the X, a handy self-feeding down supply system. Released down will ride the current and reveal the path your scent is following.

Larry R. Nelson & Thomas E. Isley
Rochester, Minnesota

Tape the swivels on your rifle sling to the stock to keep noise down.

Tape the muzzle shut to keep dust out, and install scope covers.

Keep shells in reach, but don't let them rattle (use a cartridge belt, stock sock, etc.).

Scott Karge
Muncy Valley, Pennsylvania

Apply WD-40 to sling swivels to reduce squeaking.

Don Ramsden
Winona, Minnesota

SCENTS

Elk have us backed clean off the map when it comes to sense of smell. But you can make up for your handicap by adding to your store of knowledge and gear.

Scent can be an effective way to help "cover" our own human aroma and it can be useful in arousing the curiosity of a love-lusted bull. The problem is cow-in-heat urine and bull urine can be messy to deal with while in the woods. I have found an excellent method for packing scent into the woods and keeping it contained until you really need it. I use tampons soaked in the appropriate urine and then I place them in a photo film container with the string hanging out. When I find a good set-up I can then simply pull it out of my pack, tie it onto a tree limb or whatever using the string. I don't get any on my hands and when I need to move on I simply put it back in the sealed film container. Strange, but very handy.

Mitchell Caldwell
Mount Angel, Oregon

This may sound crazy, but it has worked for me over and over again! Either still hunting or on a stand, in my hunting jacket pocket, I carry a small empty can, like sterno, inside a protective wicker holder. In the can I light punk wood, and it smokes continuously, covering my scent. The animals are used to smoke in the forest, and I have had them come to my call from downwind! The punk wood is easy to find in orangish rotting logs. It will take a few tries to find punk wood that is just right—not too hard and not too decomposed—and will keep smoking all day long. To prevent pocket fires, line the pocket with fireproof material available from any tent maker.

Roman "Dead-eye" Dodson
North Hills, California

Avoid taking the smells of elk camp into the woods. Most hunters throw on their hunting duds first thing out of the sack every morning. Next they fix breakfast. If breakfast includes preparing things like bacon, sausage and eggs, etc. you can bet that the odor gets all over the clothing that the hunter is about to wear while trying to go undetected in the woods. The same goes for lunch and supper.

Following are scent cover-up secrets that work for me:

1. Rinse all hunting clothes in the washing

machine with baking soda and place together in a plastic bag after drying.

2. About 3 to 4 days before the start of the hunt, I take chlorophyll pills three times a day and continue to do so for the duration of the hunt.

3. For my last shower before the hunt, I wash with unscented soap.

4. I wash my sweaty areas with unscented baby wipes. I store the wipes in plastic bags to keep them from drying out.

Steve Wilde
Castle Rock, Colorado

Bring your hunting duds to camp sealed in a clean plastic trash bag. Leave them there until after the morning meal preparation and clean up. When you come back to camp, whether at midday or evening, off with the hunting duds and back in the bag. This will help to keep camp odors off your hunting duds. If the sausage and eggs smelled good to you while it was cooking, you can bet it will smell the same to the elk. Leave camp odor at camp.

Jay Houston
Colorado Springs, Colorado

Your best chance is the first day on stand because coming and going leaves scent on shrubs, ground, etc. Collect pine sap from an old tree or stump with a knife and store it in a zip-locked bag. Open the bag at your hunting area for a no-cost, all-natural scent cover. This works especially well in warm weather often encountered during some early seasons. There are no glass or plastic bottles to break or leave, either.

Mike Zimmerman
Houston, Texas

❧

Scent is the bow hunter's worst enemy. I do several things to combat it. When going to a "dry" camp I always bring along all the water I can for bathing. I try to bathe every day with a no-scent soap. I wear one of the various antibacterial scent guards under my arms. I hang my hunting clothes outside of the wall tent at night so they don't pick up cooking odors and they can air out overnight. I will soak a couple of small rags in cow elk urine and pin them to my clothing during the day. Despite all the precautions, I may still get winded, but I know I've done my best to combat it.

Jeff Keller
Bend, Oregon

❧

Air currents carrying your human scent can play havoc with a stalk on a bull elk. Being in the guide business I hear horror stories constantly about how the bull "somehow" got my wind and "blew out!" A simple remedy: use a small squeeze bottle filled with powdered carpenter chalk. I carry one in my hand constantly while bow hunting and guiding elk hunters. Just give a little squeeze and puff some dust into the air. Sometimes the air flow direction will surprise you. I have had to "run away" from some bulls to keep from getting winded by them. I wouldn't hunt elk without my duster.

Al Marohn
Pickett, Wisconsin

I will use manufactured masking scents and lures, but I prefer natural scents collected where I'm hunting. I apply no-scent to my pits and through my hair, and strip the needles off spruce boughs and grind them into an odoriferous pulp between the palms of my hands, rubbing the residue into my camo. Sometimes I'll pop pitch pockets off fir and spruce by grinding a sleeve, back or leg against them. My wife isn't crazy about the idea, but she isn't a bow hunter. I also wash my camo in UV blocker detergent and bathe with unscented soap. I keep my hunting clothes in a black plastic garbage bag with green spruce boughs. I keep my fanny pack clean and my bow and arrows wiped off. Extreme measures? Bow hunting for elk calls for extreme measures. If you're lucky, you get one chance, one shot. Maybe at the next world's record. His nostrils are flaring, testing odors in the air. Is he smelling breakfast at the greasy spoon? Stepped-in horse manure from the camp meadow? Residue on your pants from a midnight stroll through the hunting camp pee patch? The stogie your partner smoked on the long drive up the mountain?

Bill Sansom
St. Regis, Montana

Whether scouting or hunting, when I find an elk bed, I pick up some of the soiled dirt and apply it to my boots and pant legs for cover scent. This has worked wonderfully.

Don Ramsden
Winona, Minnesota

When you are in the woods hunting and you come across a pile of deer or elk droppings, you should step in them, rub your boots in them really good. This will help cover your own scent and perhaps attract the game.

Jack E. Cox
San Jose, California

Save that stinkbelly! What's a stinkbelly? It's the most effective means I've ever seen of camouflaging your human smell. The next time you or your hunting buddy are fortunate enough to kill a bull elk, save that oblong patch of discolored hair located on his belly directly ahead of his calf-making tool. Cut it into one-inch-wide strips, seal it in a plastic bag and put it in the freezer until next year. When next hunting season rolls around, thaw it out and tie a strip to the outside of each pants leg. When you are putting the stalk on that bull up on the side of a mountain and breezes are swirling every which direction, a stinkbelly will maybe give you that additional edge you need to bag that trophy bull.

Jim Linnell
Ft. Worth, Texas

Do not disturb anything around your hunting area. Leave it as it was when you showed up. In other words, "Don't stink it up!"

Scott Karge
Muncy Valley, Pennsylvania

TRACKING

Whether you're trying to find an animal, or trying to find your way, these ideas can help you stay the course.

It can be difficult at times to determine in which direction elk are traveling in deep, fresh snow. If you cannot see the hoofprint, insert your hand into the track to feel in which direction the hooves are pointed.

Gaylynn "Griz" Becker
Bismarck, North Dakota

When tracking a wounded animal after dark, using a Coleman lantern, put aluminum foil around ⅔ of the glass sides. This will direct more light to the ground and in front of you while keeping the bright light from your eyes.

Don Ramsden
Winona, Minnesota

When an elk track starts meandering, it means the animal is probably looking for a bedding spot. If you're following the track, slow down and look around.

Richard E. Bennett
Bigfork, Montana

In tracking game, perhaps the most important consideration is the proper use of light. Ideally, the tracks should be between the tracker and the sun, but you can learn to position yourself to one side or the other of the tracks to take best advantage of the light. You can even track by looking back over your shoulder into the light to better see the sign you are following. If using artificial light such as a flashlight, you should use a soft or diffused beam and hold the light at a very low angle to best view the sign.

Charles N. Pirtle
Las Cruces, New Mexico

I am a bow hunter, and my hunting partner and I finally realized something, after seeing it happen several times in the past: The hunter that shoots an animal is not the better tracker—the other partner is. The hunter that releases the arrow has too much on his mind, and is still excited from the adrenaline rush of getting a good shot. The shooter also is worried about finding the animal and emotions can cloud his mind in regard to properly tracking the wounded animal. Get your partner, as he comes in with a clearer mind and is probably going to be the better tracker. We realized this year that in almost all our successful hunts the non-shooter was by far the best tracker.

Sally Bayliss
Roseburg, Oregon

A smart way to track a wounded animal which may only be bleeding slightly is to stay off to the side of the bloodrail and only proceed when the next sign of blood is found. This way you are not mixing up the trail the animal has left. If you need to backtrack, the trail of blood will still be visible. Press forward slowly, constantly checking ahead as the animal may be in view not far ahead of you. Try to sound like another animal, preferably another elk as you are moving forward; this may help you get close enough for a kill shot. Use extreme caution, as the animal may still be alive.

Reginald Brooks
Saskatoon, Saskatchewan

If you hit an animal late in the evening and it gets too dark to follow the blood trail, go back to camp and get your lantern. It will make the blood look fluorescent and hopefully lead to a harvested animal.

Rick Seymour
Glenwood Springs, Colorado

When trying to tell a bull elk track from a cow elk track, look for a track that is somewhat flat in the front of the hoof. Nine times out of ten this will be a mature bull elk. Older, bigger bulls tend to get a little lazy and drag their front feet, causing the hoof to wear down flat in front. This is a trick I learned from my grandmother, and I won lots of bets when I was guiding.

Barney Hammond
Calhan, Colorado

Instead of flagging a blood trail with orange surveyor's tape, which a lot of people will leave in the woods, I use a single sheet of single-ply toilet paper. If left in the woods it will disintegrate very quickly and no one will know you were ever there.

Jeff Keller
Bend, Oregon

When using surveyors' flagging tape to mark a route, tie your knots the same way and at the same height. This makes them easy to identify as yours. Also remember to pick them up on the way out.

Butch Grusing
Fountain, Colorado

A good trail marker for going to your stand or other particular spot is large thumbtacks and some reflective tape. Tack the tape to trees along the way to your destination. As you shine your flashlight upon the trees, the reflective tape will jump out at you and show you the way. Remove them at the end of the hunt, or the end of the season.

Reginald Brooks
Saskatoon, Saskatchewan

When you shoot an elk across a canyon, especially in new territory, you don't always have a direct route across the canyon. This can cause problems, because everything looks different when you finally get across, and your elk can be difficult to locate. I have found it helpful to mark the spot that I have taken the shot from with orange fluorescent trail tape. Then try to pick out a tree or rock, or other large landmark close to where your elk has gone down. It's amazing how much quicker you can get your bearings on the other side, if you have a bright orange reference point to look back on. Just to set the record straight, I'm not advocating long-range shooting, but this has happened to us at ranges of 250 yards or less.

Dwayne Mehrer
Okanagan Falls, British Columbia

RIFLES AND CARTRIDGES

*From the sometimes conflicting advice on the best rifles
and cartridges for elk, you can still gather thoughts and
information to help you decide what's best for you.
Whatever rifle you choose, you'll find pointers here on
how to make the best use of it.*

Many hunters feel they need to shoot magnum rifles
to hunt elk. But how many hunters can shoot magnum rifles well? Not many. Placing your shot well is
more important. I shoot a Remington 700 Mountain
Rifle in .30-06. This is a lightweight rifle, easy to pack
around. Right out of the box it's the most accurate rifle I own. It's a little too much rifle for most hunters.
I wouldn't recommend any caliber lighter than .270.
Any bullet in .270 caliber does a good job on elk and
most people can shoot a .270 pretty good. I'm a firm
believer in heavy bullets, 180 grains and up. Use a
good hunting bullet like the Speer Grand Slam, the
Nosler Partition, or the Barnes bullet. I use a 200
grain Grand Slam or Nosler Partition bullet.

Richard Robinson
Washington, Utah

There is absolutely no substitute for being competent with your rifle. Foot-pounds and fancy scopes will not make up for sloppy shooting. It makes no difference if you shoot a .243 or a .458, shoot it well and put that first shot in the lungs.

Tory Taylor
Dubois, Wyoming

There is no substitute for knock-down power. While middle caliber rifles are adequate for elk, the larger magnums are the only way to go when hunting elk. Well placed first shots may be the only shot you get in heavy cover and more elk are lost than anyone knows because of poor shot placement or lack of knock-down power. Heavier bullets possess greater knock-down power. Heavy bullets may also be an advantage when hunting heavy brush. A 220 grain elk bullet doesn't deflect or detour as much as a lighter bullet when on its way to the target. If you like the greater muzzle speed of lighter bullets but at the same time want the heavier grain bullets, load the magazine of your rifle in alternating order, depending upon your hunting conditions, i.e., heavy grain, lighter grain, heavy grain, lighter grain, etc. Carry both loads in your backup ammo, too.

Dick Taylor
Oregon City, Oregon

Elk are tough. Use the largest cartridge you can shoot accurately and are comfortable with. Elk are a big target, but a super-accurate rifle gives you confidence. The .338 Winchester Magnum is arguably the ultimate all-around elk rifle.

Richard E. Bennett
Bigfork, Montana

Elk are a big animal. Therefore, a bigger cartridge is better. I believe that a .30 caliber rifle delivers the necessary energy and velocity needed to bring down a big bull quickly. A .300 mag or a .338 mag make superb elk rifles.

Trevor Yochum
Lewiston, Idaho

The smart hunter uses a caliber big enough to get the job done. It's a sad thing when an elk is wounded because too small a caliber was used. But even the careful expert can wound an elk with a magnum. Shooting too quick and not placing your shot will wound elk, too. All the experts have their favorite elk caliber, but when it's all said and done, that old .30-06 with a partition bullet is real hard to beat. Take your time and place your shot.

Jack Lutch
Wickenburg, Arizona

When you go on that hunt of a lifetime, bring and use the same gun that you have used for years or that you are comfortable with. As a guide, I don't know how many times hunters showed up in camp with a brand new weapon that they hadn't used except to sight in. Many think that the old trusty .270 and .308 are too small for mule deer and elk. It is my opinion that a little too light of caliber is better than shooting something that is too big or that you're not used to that causes you to flinch when you pull the trigger.

Barney Hammond
Calhan, Colorado

Elk hunting costs money. For a high quality hunt with a good chance of a trophy bull, the costs might be in the thousands. Don't take a chance on being left on the sidelines while your buddies are hunting. Carry a spare rifle. It is cheap insurance. Rifles are mechanically simple devices but they do malfunction. Scopes are delicate optical instruments. That long and hazardous trip in the belly of an aircraft is not nearly as risky as the baggage handlers on both ends of the flight. An iron sighted rifle might be a good choice for a backup. If the weather turns particularly nasty, the non-optic sights might become the firearm of choice. At least one member of the party should be packing a spare. It might become the eight-pound decision that saves the hunt for someone.

Grady E. McCright
Las Cruces, New Mexico

Write the drop distances for your caliber and bullet weight on a piece of tape, and put the tape on your gunstock.

Rick Seymour
Glenwood Springs, Colorado

To prevent firing mechanisms from freezing up (with safety in mind first), dry fire the weapon. Then fully cycle safety, trigger and bolt mechanisms. This should be done prior to the start of each day's hunt and periodically during the day if conditions warrant.

Save some time and money by zeroing your rifle at 25 yards before moving it to 100 yards. Use a half-inch dot at 25 yards. When you are hitting a half inch below the dot at 25 yards, you will be ready for 100 yards. You will need little adjustment at 100 yards. Be sure to shoot at 100 yards to finalize your zero.

Daniel Nelson
Mesa, Arizona

Rifles and Cartridges

Practice shooting water-filled milk jugs to improve your shooting skills. It's fun, and spectacularly demonstrates the power of a bullet. Be sure to clean up afterwards. Shoot from different positions, including standing. You don't find many benches when you're out hunting, so try using other things as a rest, such as a backpack, post or chair.

Mike Mobbs
Olympia, Washington

When hunting in rain, snow or mud I always cover the muzzle of my barrel with a single strip of electrical tape. This will keep debris out of the barrel in case I slip or fall. The tape does not have to be removed prior to firing the rifle and does not effect the accuracy of the gun.

Lynn Talley
Hobbs, New Mexico

Much of the time I carry my rifle by the sling over my shoulder, leaving the barrel pointing upward. When it's raining or snowing I place a small balloon over the barrel of my rifle. Keeping moisture out of the barrel will prevent rust and keep a rifle in better long-term condition. Firing through the balloon is no problem.

Dick Taylor
Oregon City, Oregon

An old standard: to prevent debris, snow, etc., from accumulating in the bores: Place a piece of tape over the muzzle. This does not affect bullet impact as gasses exiting the muzzle blow the tape away before the bullet exits.

Daniel Nelson
Mesa, Arizona

This is an old tip, but one that I have only rarely seen used: To keep my rifle barrel dry during rainstorms, to keep dust and grit out, and to prevent blockage of my barrel due to snow or mud (in case I slip, or drop my gun) I place a piece of electrical tape over the end of my barrel. A more frequently appreciated advantage of the tape is gained by placing the end of a 10- to 12-inch piece of brightly colored sewing thread underneath it. This will show you at a glance the precise wind direction, without scaring game by sifting dust through your hands, or flicking a lighter.

Jay D. Williams
Nampa, Idaho

Put a piece of black electrical tape over your rifle muzzle to keep out snow, rain or mud. It won't affect accuracy and you won't have to worry about cleaning your bore. Just don't use the inexpensive tape, it won't hold up in cold weather.

Randall Tlachac
Plymouth, Minnesota

Who hasn't stumbled in the field and jammed some mud or snow in their rifle barrel? Well, here's a simple field cleaner that's easy to make, costs next to nothing and weighs even less. Take a nylon cleaning tip of the appropriate caliber, cut the threaded part off and drill a hole in the base. Next glue in the base a heavy piece of monofilament (I used weedeater line). Be sure to use a good glue which will truly bond the cleaning tip to the monofilament. Coil it up and throw it in your day pack with a couple of patches. The line is stiff enough to feed through the barrel. Grab the end when it comes out and pull the rag through to clean your barrel out in a jiffy.

Scott Campbell
Colorado Springs, Colorado

If you're a reloader that uses a hand primer, getting the primers in the tray is hard with the new large safety packaging. Just take a plastic bowl lid and punch a hole just inside the lip large enough for the primer to fall through. Then dump the required number of primers into the lid, then tip the lid to let the primers fall through the hole into the primer tray.

Elk Hunting Secrets   58

If you use a case tumbler or vibrator to clean your cases, try adding a squirt of Soft Scrub and a squirt of Brasso to the cleaning compound. It will take all but the worst stains off the brass and leave it silky smooth.

Mike Moore
Lincoln, Nebraska

If reloading, work up a safe, accurate load, not a high power load, usually 5 grains below maximum.

Scott Karge
Muncy Valley, Pennsylvania

When sighting in your rifle on a bench, rest the forestock on bags of sand for stability, to eliminate "human error." Shoot groups of 3 to 5 rounds at 25 yards, adjusting your scope until you have a satisfactory group of hits about an inch below the bull's eye, which should be your aim point at distances out to at least 200 yards for most rifles. (For longer-range shooting, you must aim above the point where you want your bullet to hit—consult ballistics tables for your particular rifle and ammunition to know how high you must hold at longer ranges.) Move to 100 yards and adjust your scope to hit dead on the bull's eye, or a little high, depending on your particular rifle and load. Again, try to shoot a tight group, reducing barrel movement as much as possible, so you know where your gun will actually put the bullets if you do your part well. Move to 200 yards and shoot more 3- to 5-round groups. Repeat until satisfied with your performance. If you can't keep your bullets in a tight group (say, 4 inches) from a bench rest at any given yardage, you're likely to spray them out of the kill zone at the same yardage under field conditions, resulting in a wounded animal. Limit your shots to those within your ability. Start with a clean rifle bore. For at least your final round of shooting at the range, use the same ammunition you'll be using on the hunt. Use ear plugs and muffs at the range to prevent permanent hearing loss.

John R. Harvieux
Balsam Lake, Wisconsin

To ensure accuracy:
- Be aware of several essential elements of a good shooting position. Try to allow the bone structure of your body, not muscular tension, to support the rifle. The left, or forward arm should be as near vertical as possible to support the fore end of the rifle. Relax the muscles of that arm as much as is practical. Steady relaxation is vital.

The trigger hand (usually the right hand) should grasp the stock with a firm, steady grip. The right arm is immobilized once the butt of the rifle is in the pocket of the shoulder.

A snug fit between cheek and the stock must be made to make your head and the rifle one unit. This is called spot-weld. Avoid canting the rifle as this will throw the strike of the bullet off target, no matter what type of sight you use.

Breath control is very important to get that bullet where you want it. Inhaling and exhaling will raise and lower your point of aim depending on which position you are in. Ideally, before a shot you should take a breath and let it out normally, letting the crosshairs come to rest on the target (the exact spot the bullet should go) at the same moment when all your breath has been exhaled. At this point there is a natural pause in breathing which is the most relaxed state possible. This is when you squeeze the trigger. Another, less desirable method is to release your breath until you are on target, then hold your breath and squeeze.

The offhand position is difficult to master. I think the most common error is the use of the left (front) arm. If your arm is extended and tensely grabbing the fore piece of the stock you are not using the support arm correctly. The upper arm should rest on the rib cage. Pull the left elbow up, across and then let it sit down on the bones. The lower arm extends straight vertically up from your chest to support the rifle right under the receiver. I like to put the trigger guard in the rear of the pocket of my palm and extend my fingers along the underside of the stock. In other words, the rifle sits in my hand like it is on a platform. The rifle is bone-supported from my shoulder and held steady. Remaining in controlled relaxation is now the key to a well-placed shot.

It is a good idea to practice, or dry fire, in various positions including awkward ones that you might find yourself in while hunting. Can you shoot while stooped over, crouching or squatting down? Supported positions are when you rest the rifle on branches, rocks, mounds, etc. These are good to use, but make sure nothing touches the barrel of the rifle.

If you do not pull the trigger gently, you will completely blow everything else you have done up until now. The trigger should be squeezed slowly and steadily straight to the rear until the shot is fired. When the sights leave the point of aim the squeeze is ceased and begun again when the sights are once again steady on the target.

When using a scope, it is important to maintain proper eye relief. (To determine proper eye relief, see tip from Daniel Nelson in the Optics section of this book. Page 90)

The field of view should be clear, circular, and free of any shadows. If a shadow is visible on any side of the scope, the bullet will tend to strike off the point of aim, in the direction opposite the shadow.

- How far away is that bull? Range estimation is a very important skill which must be developed by practice. Visit your local football field and pace off the hundred yards. Practice estimating the distance to targets or other objects out in the field, and then pace the distance off to see how close you were with your estimate. For distances up to 400 yards, try to see how many 100 yard increments you can place between yourself and the target. For distances

over 400, choose a spot halfway and then estimate the distance to that spot. Double that
range and that is the distance to the target.

Some helpful hints when estimating range:

- Looking downhill, the target appears closer.
- Looking uphill, the target appears farther
  away.
- Looking across a draw or depression which is
  entirely visible makes the target appear more
  distant.
- When the draw or depression is not visible,
  such as a gorge, the target appears closer than
  it actually is.
- A target appears closer when it stands out from
  the surroundings. The target will seem farther
  when it blends in with the surroundings.
- In bright light from the hunter's rear, the target seems closer.
- At dawn or dusk or poorly lighted conditions,
  the target appears farther away.

Whenever possible, obtain maps of the area you
are going to hunt in and write down ranges from
various sets of points. For example, figure out the
ranges from ridge to drainage floor and from one
ridge to the next ridge in the area. Determine ranges
from prominent landmarks to other landmarks in
the hunting ground to serve as guides when estimating distances to your quarry.

Hold-off is a correction in the aiming point to
compensate for the bullet's trajectory at ranges other
than the range for which the rifle is zeroed at. A rifle
is zeroed at 100 yards when the bullet fired from a

distance of 100 yards strikes the point on the target where the sights rest. With most rifles, if you are zeroed for 100 yards, you have to aim high if shooting a deer at 400 yards. As a guide to vertical measurement at the target, use an 18-inch scale for deer and a 24-inch scale for elk. This is an average depth from brisket to backbone of these animals.

Corrections in aiming point for the wind are sometimes important also. The shooter must aim into the wind to compensate for wind velocity. If the wind is blowing from your left, aim left of the target a little bit, and vice versa. A general rule to figure out how far to aim into the wind is given by $R \times \frac{V}{15}$, where R equals the range in hundreds of yards, V equals wind velocity and 15 is a constant. A wind of 1-3 mph can barely be felt. Smoke drifts slowly by. A wind of 3-5 mph can be felt lightly on the face. A wind of 5-8 mph causes leaves on trees to be in constant motion, tall grasses sway. A wind of 8-12 mph raises dust and small debris. A wind 12-15 mph causes small trees to sway. Winds at right angles to the line of fire are full value; winds at oblique angles are half-value. For half value winds the aiming point is only adjusted half as much as for a full value wind. The best way to get used to the wind and its effect on the bullet is to shoot on a range many times in different wind conditions.

Shannon Bolton
Lolo, Montana

MUZZLELOADERS

Keep your powder dry. Among other things.

In order to keep good accuracy, the powder has to be packed tightly in a black powder gun. Everyday I take the ramrod and put it in the muzzle. Then I take the ½-by-6-inch starter rod and tap the ramrod down. You can feel the powder charge tighten up. Be very careful; take the cap off when you do this. Otherwise you could lose some fingers.

Mark Hnatiuk
San Antonio, Texas

Believe it or not, flintlock muzzleloaders can be more reliable in wet weather than a percussion rifle. Why? Because if you get water inside your percussion, you can't very easily get it out, but with a flintlock it's easy. Here is my tip for how to "keep your powder dry" (the *ffff* powder in your pan, that is): Take equal amounts of beeswax and patch lube and melt them together in an old pot, then pour the mixture into empty film canisters. After it cools, you have a small container of waxy paste to keep in your possibles bag. After loading your gun, prime the pan as usual with *ffff* powder. Then use a small amount of your wax mixture to seal the seams between the frizzen and the pan, and Presto! Waterproof! Do not open the pan during the day to check your powder, as this will allow moisture to get in. I have been using this technique for 10 years now, and have killed an elk, a black bear and two deer after hunting most of the day during the rain.

Paul Noon
Hamburg, Pennsylvania

You know the old saying, "Keep your powder dry." I keep mine dry in my muzzleloader by putting a piece of black tape over the end of the barrel and one over the nipple. When I get a shot opportunity, I only have to flip off the tape on the nipple and just shoot right through the tape on the end of the barrel.

Bill Steinbach
Boise, Idaho

Keep your powder dry. After preparing individual charges or loads use a food vacuum sealer to keep out moisture.

Dan Nelson
Mesa, Arizona

Always carry a bottle of clear fingernail polish. When the weather is wet, swab the polish around the nipple. After drying, it will seal for sure fire. After 20 years of hunting with the smoke pole, I've had a lot of misfires, but only when I left the bottle at home.

Tim Sattler
Yakima, Washington

Using a peep sight on muzzleloaders will help accuracy for target shooting, but stay with open sights for moving shots in dim light.

Jack Yates
Bartlett, Tennessee

One challenge of hunting with a muzzleloader is ramrod containment on the rifle. Securing the ramrod with electrical or duct tape wrapped around both barrel and rod remedies the situation. Remember to fold over the end of the tape so it can be quickly removed.

To prevent loss of a muzzleloader capping tool, place it on a lanyard attached to a shirt button hole or belt loop. Make sure the lanyard is of sufficient length to allow capping of the rifle while capper is fastened to lanyard. Practice this technique before your hunt.

Dan Nelson
Mesa, Arizona

With black powder rifles, as with bows, you need a personal yardage limit. Mine is 100 yards. Elk are big and tough. I personally will not hunt elk with a muzzleloader with less than .54 caliber and less than 425 grain bullets.

Richard E. Bennett
Big Fork, Montana

BOWS AND ARROWS

Practice plenty, know your yardage limit, and . . . .

When shooting at an elk you have to block out the antlers completely. It's real easy to miss a bull when you're half focused on the vitals and half focused on the antlers. Pick out a piece of ruffled hair or something of that manner that sticks out on the bull. Make sure it is right behind the front shoulder and in the middle of the body. Instead of simply aiming at the chosen spot, what I do is come to full draw and aim at the back side of the front leg about knee level. Then slowly follow the leg up until you reach your chosen spot and release the arrow. This will make you focus more and make you more accurate. It also works well for long-range shots with a rifle.

Rick French
Wasilla, Alaska

When bow hunting, think heavy arrows. The light 3D arrows are better left at home. Heavy arrows and broadheads will help your bow to be quieter, and easier to tune for good flight. Heavy arrows also enable a bow at a given draw weight to increase kinetic energy for added penetration. It is much better to shoot heavy arrows than to increase draw weight so much it's difficult to draw your bow. The carbon shafts will also help with penetration as long as they are tuned for the individual, and have adequate weight.

If you're now using feather fletching on your arrows, try some of the new plastic vanes. They are lighter than the ones used previously and the benefits outweigh the added weight. They will allow you to hunt in the rain or snow and they will be quieter in the brush.

A hip quiver is best when hunting. It's easier to get through the brush, and the bow doesn't get as heavy after a day of mountain climbing.

Tom Morava
Rushville, Nebraska

You need a personal yardage limit—mine is thirty yards.

Richard E. Bennett
Bigfork, Montana

Don't *begin* practicing with your bow—shoot it *all year* at targets, 3D shoots and archery leagues. Practice with the same tackle you hunt with. That means with bow quiver attached and full of arrows, stabilizer in place, and shooting broadheads. Hold your bow at full draw for a ten count, building to a twenty count before you release. This helps you mentally talk yourself through the shot, and builds your strength. Shoot from varied distances, angles, elevations and positions. If you hunt out of a tree stand, practice out of one. Use your practice arrows for practice, saving the rest for the hunt. Change your razor inserts prior to the hunt, or resharpen your broadheads. Store your bow out of heat and sunlight, preferably in a bow case, so it won't detune. Have your pro shop regularly check and tune your bow, and straighten and spin match your arrows to your broadheads. Practice with a knowledgeable partner that can observe your shooting technique. Shoot every practice shot as if you were shooting at a once-in-a-lifetime bull.

Bill Sansom
St. Regis, Montana

To keep from losing expensive bow releases, I use a plastic "coiled chain" with a snap. It looks like a phone cord and costs only a buck or so. One end is tied to my release and the other is snapped to a belt loop on my hip. The cord stays out of the way and will always have my $40 release attached to the end of it.

Al Marohn
Pickett, Wisconsin

In September it can be pretty hot and dry, which makes moving around in the woods quietly very difficult. I will put on four pair of wool boot socks and sneak around in them. The wool will even muffle the sound of dry pine needles and by wearing four pair my feet don't take a beating if I happen to step on an occasional rock.

Jeff Keller
Bend, Oregon

A team of two works well when archery elk hunting. Move through the forest within sight of each other, cow calling with occasional bugles. This will sound much more like an elk herd and if someone gets an opportunity for a shot, the other person can cow call to distract the elk.

Todd Corsetti
Pocatello, Idaho

I arrange my arrows in my bow quiver so that all the cock feathers are indexed the same and I do not have to look at my arrow as I nock it. To do this, install one arrow on the string in the normal fashion and when removing it, hold it firmly and install it into the quiver. Then simply place the other arrows indexed the same as the cock feather. This allows for much quicker follow-up shots.

I have had two small pockets sewn onto all of my hunting shirts and coats so that my cow calls on lanyards are in one pocket and my compact binoculars are in the other and neither are interfering with my bow string and always available for immediate use.

Alan Johnson
Rapid City, South Dakota

With bow hunting gaining popularity, hunters need to set a new standard of ethics. Shot placement is very important, so limit your shooting distance. Elk will jump the string no matter how fast your bow is. My personal limit is 40 yards.

Trevor Yochum
Lewiston, Idaho

When I bow hunt elk in early September, I'm always on the lookout for mushrooms in the dark timber. The elk around here seem to really go for them, and I plan my hunting trip around a nice little drainage that I've nicknamed "Mushroom Draw," due to the abundance of mushrooms found there. When the mushrooms start popping up, the elk are soon to follow.

Greg Becker
Victor, Idaho

CALLS AND CALLING

*Don't overdo it, and don't worry if you don't sound
like the Godzilla of bull elk.*

Many people have a hard time with diaphragms, but
they make some good calls with the diaphragm attached to the grunt tube. Use what is easy for you.
Don't be intimidated by people that sound better
than you. Elk all have different personalities and
voices. I don't feel that I'm a great sounding caller,
but I call a lot of bulls in. Some of the bulls don't
sound as good as I do. I called a bull in last September that sounded so bad he needed to take some les-
sons himself. If the bull doesn't come in, don't take
it personal, there are a lot of reasons why a bull
won't come in that have nothing to do with you.
Just keep downwind and leave the area quietly without being seen. You can try for him another day.

Richard Robinson
Washington, Utah

When bugling, don't expect elk to come at you on a full trot. One of the biggest and wariest bulls I ever guided a hunter to stalked us like a tiger. Had the 6x7 approached us from downwind or had he seen us first as he snuck through bushy whitebark pine, he would have vanished without us knowing he was there. This bull never gave a peep in response to my bugles.

Tory Taylor
Dubois, Wyoming

My bugle is so puny sounding that I'd get laughed right off the stage at one of those elk bugling contests. But my stage is the snow slide chutes and black spruce of the timberline basins. I'm not trying to impress any judges, or show off my ferocity. I want to sound like a 98-pound weakling, waiting for some bully to stomp over and kick wallow mud in my face, and take my girl away from me. Quite a few have tried. They've wound up in my freezer, and on my wall.

Bill Sansom
St. Regis, Montana

When you're calling during archery season, often-times the elk will come in and hang up. Make sure the elk isn't looking at you or in your direction. Then turn your head and cover your mouth with your hand part way and cow call. This makes the call sound like it's coming from a false location and the elk won't pinpoint your exact location.

Rick French
Wasilla, Alaska

The only call I use is a cow call. It is not a diaphragm call, so I wear it on a small lanyard around my neck so I always know where it is and can retrieve it quickly. When I'm still hunting or on a stand and elk appear but aren't coming my direction, I use the call to halt their drifting and keep them milling around looking for the cow I'm imitating. Usually, if the elk are not spooked, they will stay in the area while I try for a better position.

Dick Taylor
Oregon City, Oregon

When hunting in heavily hunted areas, make calls as real as possible. Elk are much smarter than most people think. They know where the roads are, what vehicles sound like and the difference between a real sounding bugle and an imitation. Past experiences from hunting in heavily hunted areas and perfecting my calling to sound as real as possible have helped

me bring bulls in closer where otherwise they might
have never returned a call.

Trevor Yochum
Lewiston, Idaho

When cow calling, we chirp through our bugle tubes.
Maybe others do this as well, but I've never seen it
done or read about it. The bugle tube gives the cow
calls more resonance and realism. We've called in otherwise reluctant cows, calves and bulls this way.

I learned this next pointer from hunting turkey
gobblers in the spring. It sure seems to help in pre-
venting bulls from getting "hung up" when they
are coming to the call. Set up where trees, brush or
rock create a barrier big enough to hide the "elk"
that the real elk think they hear, especially when
challenging a rutting bull. It seems if the bull re-
sponding to the hunter's calling can see the area
from which the calls are coming, but (should be
able to and) can't see the elk supposedly issuing the
challenge, the bull oftentimes "hangs up" or stops
his approach out of range (especially with bow and
arrow); however, if the hunter is behind some type
of barrier through which the elk can't see and
which is big enough to hide a real elk, the elk coming to the call will approach close enough to see
through or around the barrier and present a good,
close-range shot.

Scott Beal
Rapid City, South Dakota

If hunting in a group, be sure you know the sound of your fellow hunters' bugles so that you don't waste time doing a sneak on your buddy.

Todd Corsetti
Pocatello, Idaho

An excellent, simple call to construct which rates up there with the best store-bought calls can be made by a pop bottle and a vacuum cleaner hose.

1. Cut the top of a 500 ml plastic pop bottle off to fit tightly into the end of the hose (leave lid on).
2. Drill a ⅜-inch hole into the plastic lid just so the edge of the ⅜-inch hole is very near the edge of the cap.
3. Lightly stretch a piece of light latex over ⅔ of the hole, leaving ⅓ nearest the edge of the lid for air flow. This latex may be fastened on by an "O" ring over the lid or a simple elastic band.
4. You may have to fool a bit with the latex to achieve the proper notes and tones. They will come a runnin'!

Next time an elk refuses to come into range, try turning and blowing your call directly behind you and try to make him believe the elk which was once close has moved further away. This may make the elk press forward and pass the shooter for a shot.

Reginald Brooks
Saskatoon, Saskatchewan

You can spend a lot of money on bugles and calls but with a little practice, you can do the same thing with your fingers. This includes the cow call, too. Just learn to blow.

Jack Lutch
Wickenburg, Arizona

Choose a hidden spot to do your bugling. Elk are very smart and have unbelievable homing ability. On a number of occasions I have bugled at elk that were a good distance away and had them come within 15 yards or less and stop, look for the other bull and stay in place looking, but not go any farther. These animals are a hell of a lot smarter than some people give them credit for.

Elk will "shut up" and not bugle when hunters do a lot of "bad judgment" bugling. Nothing irritates me more than pictures or videos that show someone right out in the open bugling (sometimes even on horseback). Any kind of "elk calling" should be done under cover. That is if you want that bull to come within a reasonable distance.

Brian Taylor
Kelly, Wyoming

Call with a cow call calmly and cautiously—don't overdo it. Two or three times every 10 to 20 minutes is enough.

Scott Karge
Muncy Valley, Pennsylvania

OPTICS

With almost as many options in optics as in weapons, you'll just have to weigh the opinions of our tipsters, and make your own choices.

Never hunt without binoculars.

> *Richard E. Bennett*
> *Bigfork, Montana*

I firmly believe that you should invest more money in your binoculars than in your rifle and scope combined.

> *Charles N. Pirtle*
> *Las Cruces, New Mexico*

If you hunt the timber, why carry a binocular which is made for viewing long distances? The 10X to 15X glasses now available are heavy and bulky. If small, they sacrifice field of view. A 6X or 7X binocular weighing less than a pound will be handy and convenient for glassing deadfalls and timber. The sight of a patch of elk hide at 50 yards has a better chance of leading to a trophy than the sight of an elk in the open miles away.

Gerald Westesen
Bozeman, Montana

Larger optics are the way to go, even when hunting heavy timber. Their light gathering properties will always be a benefit when trying to evaluate or identify big game.

Weight of the optics is often the excuse for compact binoculars and it's no secret that optics hung around your neck during a day afield will produce great strain and headaches by the end of the day. Early in my hunting career, I solved this problem by transferring the weight of the optics to my belt. A short length of cord, shoe string or baling twine tied to the midpoint on your optics strap and then tied to your back belt loop or belt, so that the binocular strap is held an inch or two off of your neck, will allow a hunter to hunt all day without feeling the weight of the optics. Recently I have created binocular support straps for me and a companion by separating the two straps of a pair of suspenders (the kind with the large snaps). I snap one end of the suspender strap at the midpoint on the optics strap and snap the other end of the suspender to my belt or pants in line with my spine in back. The snap makes rearranging layers or taking care of business much easier.

Dick Taylor
Oregon City, Oregon

If your vision requires correction for good distant vision, and if you despise surveying a hillside with binoculars while wearing glasses as much as I do, you are constantly removing the specs and laying them aside or gripping the ear pieces in your teeth while inspecting the terrain for game. Fearful that one day I would break, lose or walk away from my glasses when afield, I searched for a viable solution. Insurance is simple. Purchase an eyeglass lanyard and never go afield without it attached to the ear pieces and securely looped around your neck. This device also allows the rapid removal of the glasses to make that hoped-for quick shot using a scoped rifle, all the while suspending the delicate eyewear on your chest.

Grady E. McCright
Las Cruces, New Mexico

A simple piece of elastic band material bought from your nearest fabric supply store and attached to either side of your binos will help keep your binos from swinging out in front of you while bending over, etc. Attach to one side of your binos, then around your back and then to the other side of the binos.

Reginald Brooks
Saskatoon, Saskatchewan

Using a spotting scope for extended periods causes one's eyes to feel like they are about to fall from their sockets. Muscle strain causing this discomfort can be reduced by using an eye patch covering the eye not looking through the scope. To get further relief, try alternating between left and right eyes for viewing. The patch makes this easy.

To determine optimal eye relief (distance of your eye from your rifle scope) when preparing to mount a new scope on your rifle, shine a small flashlight beam through the objective lens of the scope while holding it a few inches from a wall. Move the scope towards or away from the wall until the light beam becomes focused. When the beam is focused the proper eye relief is the distance the scope is from the wall.

Daniel Nelson
Mesa, Arizona

Fixed power scopes should not be above 4-power. Never set variable power scopes above 4-power while hunting. If you take aim at an animal that is fairly close to you, all you will see is hair, and you

may not know which part of the animal you're looking at. If a long shot presents itself, you can raise the
power then.

Richard E. Bennett
Bigfork, Montana

Do your best to not bang your scope on anything. If
available, get scope mounts that enable you to use
open sights as well as your scope, in case your scope
is bumped while hunting and you can no longer be
sure of its accuracy.

Don't use your rifle scope as binoculars. It is a
"heart stopper" to your fellow hunters when they
find your rifle pointed at them, and it is very dangerous.

Butch Grusing
Fountain, Colorado

CAMPING

A few pointers on keeping camp life clean, easy,
comfortable—and civil.

I have spent most of 41 seasons hunting out of
camps. Base camps, spike camps, drop camps, fly-in
camps and KOA camps. I have adopted the following rules from breeches of etiquette I have personally
witnessed or participated in.

1. Never tie your horse to the cooktent. These
   normally docile steeds have only one
   thought on their minds: going back to the
   barn. They interpret the sudden appearance
   of the camp cook, rushing out through the
   tent flap with a frying pan full of flaming
   bacon, as a signal to immediately break
   camp and gallop off to the trailhead with
   the cooktent, and its occupants, in tow.

2. Never dump the dregs of your coffee mug
   on the dirt floor of the cooktent, or spit to-
   bacco juice or food on the floor. Not only
   in this a disgusting habit, it is a hard one to
   break once you return home.

3. Do not toss the remains of your cup, used pan of dishwater, or empty bottles out through the tent flap. Someone may have forgotten rule one. Or, someone may be entering the tent.

4. Never use your partner's coffee cup as a spittoon or chamber pot without asking him first.

5. Do not use the last of the latrine tissue and not tell anyone.

6. It is bad taste to ask to borrow someone's long underwear until yours dries.

7. Do not unduly disturb your buddy's sleep by hoarsely whispering, "Did you guys hear that?" or by asking if anyone else has ants in their sleeping bag.

8. Do not take the cot furthest from the stove, then insist on stoking the fire all night because you're cold.

9. Do not re-ignite dying embers in the sleeping tent stove by tossing in a cupful of chainsaw gas. Especially if you are using your partner's cup.

10. Never keep a loaded gun in camp. Someone could be injured. That someone would likely be the person that violated the rules.

Bill Sansom
St. Regis, Montana

If elk hunting in grizzly-sensitive areas such as the Greater Yellowstone Ecosystem, make plans to immediately pack elk to town from the kill-site and avoid bringing meat, hides or antlers into camp.

Too often, hunters new to an elk area may make the mistake of camping right in the elk. That beautiful meadow full of elk droppings makes a nice camp, but you are probably messing up the hunting for both you and other hunters.

Do-it-yourself drop camps are one of the most overlooked and potentially successful methods of elk hunting not being used today. Consider having a packer drop you at elk heaven, do your own cooking and guiding, and keep in touch with the packer by cell phone to tell him when your tag is on the elk.

Tory Taylor
Dubois, Wyoming

When you have to approach another camp, let them know you are coming. "Hello to the camp" is always a good idea and can avoid startling the campers.

Butch Grusing
Fountain, Colorado

Dampness and cold are constant challenges when in elk camp. Moist socks can be dried by body heat during the night while you are sleeping by putting the socks in the sleeping bag with you. Shirts and pants will loose their morning chill if you lay them out smoothly beneath your sleeping bag. Body warmth will have them very comfortable in the morning when you roll out and dress for the day.

Dick Taylor
Oregon City, Oregon

One of the handiest tools around camp is the camp hook, as I call it. When cooking with Dutch ovens it is almost a necessity. To remove the heavy cast lid for inspection of the contents the hook is applied to the lid handle. This works much better than a gloved hand which oftentimes becomes hot much quicker than expected, and if baking with live coals on the lipped lid, a gloved approach is downright hazardous. A small notch filed in the underside of the lid handle at the center-of-gravity facilitates this process. The hook is also useful for moving other hot utensils around on the campfire by grabbing the bail of the bucket. To construct, use ¼-inch cold-rolled steel. Apply enough heat to soften the metal and bend an ample T-handle at one end of a length of rod and a one-inch long, 135-degree V bent toward the handle at the other end. The overall length can be whatever is desired. For Dutch oven lids with coals on top, I recommend not less than 15 inches, but make several. I have one that is only six inches long that I am fond of, and the short version works better for pulling tent pegs at the conclusion of the hunt.

A very useful tool around an elk camp is an ordinary galvanized bucket. I find a two-gallon size ideal. Let the bucket get smoked up on the campfire grate and don't worry about it. I transport mine in a wooden box also containing Dutch ovens and other cast utensils. When the wood fire is burning, there is usually hot water simmering in the bucket. It is a handy way to heat dishwater. Washing your face on a cold morning is far more pleasant with warm water. I also use the bucket to transport water and collect potato peelings while preparing a meal. Try a bucket. They make good camp mates. One caution: Do not use water from a galvanized bucket for cooking or drinking.

Grady E. McCright
Las Cruces, New Mexico

Sometimes, hunting alone, I camp in my old Jeep. I take out the removable passenger seat and have a space seven feet long and almost three feet wide between the tailgate and the firewall to lay down an air mattress and two heavy sleeping bags. When camping in my Jeep I use a microwave for cooking. A microwave? You bet. That is what the jeep guys I run around with call a piece of driveline tube cut to about the length of a large can of soup or stew, with a tab welded to it so it can be bolted to an exhaust manifold. I drop a can of stew in the microwave bolted to the Chevy 327 V8 that powers my jeep, run the engine for 20 minutes, and dinner's hot and ready to eat. Drop in a potato wrapped in foil, and after a two hour's drive I enjoy a hot baked potato.

Harlan White
Canyonville, Oregon

Make all your favorite foods and freeze two days before you head out. Spaghetti is great; just heat the sauce and cook your pasta. I use elbow macaroni because it doesn't break as much.

Buy one or two gallon water containers from the local grocery, freeze, and use this for ice that won't get everything in the cooler wet. Then use for drinking water when melted.

Use old carpet for a doormat outside the tent and in the vestibule. Keep dirty boots there.

L. Minish
Highlands Ranch, Colorado

For those hunters that like to cook with wood, cut off about a 13-inch-high piece of galvanized culvert. A 3-foot-wide culvert works well, but you can use a larger size depending on the crowd. Cut a U-shaped hole on the bottom for air to feed the fire. Make the hole wide enough for a square point shovel (in case you need coals for a Dutch oven). Set the piece of culvert on bare ground and lay a grill (a piece of sandscreen works fine) across the top to cook on. Advantages are that you can cook in the wind, you don't lose any heat, and the grill is level. Cover with a piece of tin roofing when you leave camp to keep the fire pit dry.

Any camp should have hot water, and the easy way is to use a big coffee pot with a lid. The water stays clean, and you can just leave it on the grill.

For the ultimate hunting experience, you can't beat a good tent. The 9½-foot range tent (cowboy tepee) is just right for one man. I have a 14-by-16-foot wall tent, and it isn't any too big for four hunters. Use a good canvas fly at least 18 by 25 feet over the tent to keep it dry.

Jack Lutch
Wickenburg, Arizona

Many times I camp where water is sometimes hard to come by or has to be taken along. I bought a garden sprayer (the type that holds 2-3 gallons of water and is pumped by hand). I use this around camp to take a quick shower or wash dishes. It can also be used to wash off a dirty carcass. The small amount of water you will use is very surprising compared to letting most of it be wasted the old way (dipping or pouring it out of a bucket).

Dean Hendrickson
Palmdale, California

It has been my experience that horses and coffeepots with percolators just don't mix. Invariably I ended up losing the percolator or breaking the percolator cap. To me the romance of drinking "cowboy coffee" ended when I had to start picking the coffee grounds out of my teeth. The human mind being what it is a better way had to be found and I think I have. There is a product on the market that has the coffee in a sealed pouch that is normally used in the basket of drip coffee makers. I take one of these pouches and throw it in a pot and boil it till I get the color I want. It works, tastes good and no more grounds in my cup. What more would you want in a cup of coffee 20 miles from the road?

Lynn Talley
Hobbs, New Mexico

PACKING WITH HORSES AND MULES

*Ways to avoid unplanned rodeos—and protect you,
your gear, and your stock.*

Not every horse or mule can pack gear into the
mountains or game into camp. You can teach him
to pack but whether or not the animal will be trust-
worthy enough to get your gear into the mountains
safely and without mishap is up to him. I prefer
mules for two reasons. First, mules are built to pack.
The withers are more narrow than on horses and
this helps keep the load balanced. The physical at-
tributes make mules more suitable for traversing the
often rocky and treacherous terrain that lies within
the backcountry. Mules also tend to be more
surefooted than a horse. Second, most of the mules I
have worked with are better thinkers; that is, when
they get themselves into trouble they tend to think
their way out of it, whereas a horse will bust every
piece of gear on him and around him to get clear of
trouble.

A lot may be said for a short horse or mule. If the animal you are trying to pack is sixteen hands or better, imagine how difficult it will be trying to lift a hundred pound load and hold it up that high while trying to lash it to the critter. Medium build stock, 14 to 15 hands, is usually the best bet. Believe me, in the middle of the night on a steep trail you want to spend as little time as possible adjusting that loose pack.

Pick a pack animal with good disposition. Occasionally there is little choice and the "packee" may be ornery and prone to buck, but stay away from trying to convert former track racers and bucking stock; you will only be chasing him through the hills while he is dragging your gear off to the middle of nowhere.

If you are taking green stock into the hills you better have a veteran pack horse in the bunch. Tie the trainee off to the seasoned veteran. Put him up front where you can keep an eye on him, but usually the more experienced horse will keep the green horse in line. By the end of the trip the greenhorn will have a whole new understanding of work and will likely be ready for another trip soon. Try to keep the load light on the new pack animal. Duffels, sleeping bags and grain or pellets make good loads. If he forgets his manners and tries to buck off the pack, he can't hurt it or himself. No horse or mule is perfect so use your best judgment and pick the animals you get along best with and trust the most.

There is one piece of gear that you should never forget to pack in. It is the all inclusive war bag. This is simply the bag, box or pack that contains necessary tools you will need, or may need, in emergencies or to keep the string in good health. Think of it as a first-aid kit for horses. You should have a good brush, curry comb and a jar of salve. A gall from an unbalanced pack or dirty cinch can put the pack animal out of commission for the rest of the trip. Carry along extra horseshoes, nails and a file, nippers and hammer. Bring some extra rope, hobbles, cinches, bells, and some iodine. It's also a good idea to carry along some extra buckles, maybe a headstall and a halter or two. The deer that may frequent your camp in search of salt or grain are incurable kleptomaniacs and these items may come up missing. Take along a good 35-foot lariat. You may want it to drag in tent poles or firewood. Whatever you think you may need to take care of horses while on the trip, you should bring. Making the extra room in a pack will be well worth it.

A string of 10 to 20 horses can make a lot of dust stomping around. To keep this dust out of your coffee pot, locate the picket line away from camp 30 yards or more. A heavy, ratcheting, nylon line strung between a couple of stout trees will hold the string just fine. The key to harmony on the picket line is to remember the pecking order. It's the same up here as it is at home. I usually station the mules in a group by themselves which keeps the horses from pulling rank, as is often the case.

Take care of your gear daily. A good tarp is cheap insurance against marauding deer and sudden cloudbursts. Saddle blankets and packs need to ing along. The very first thing I would see of the animals is their lower legs. You almost always see the legs first, because the upper limbs screen your view, and you lean down and look under the lower limbs of the trees to see better. Those dark horses' legs look just like elk legs from back a ways in the timber. Some horse hunters I met had orange leg wraps on their horses' lower legs, which really helped me know that it was a horse and rider approaching, and not a band of elk. Some of them just spray-painted their horses' legs bright orange each day. If I had a horse in brush country I would certainly get some bright colors on it, especially low on its legs. Make them visible.

Harlan White
Canyonville, Oregon

Take care of your gear daily. A good tarp is cheap insurance against marauding deer and sudden cloudbursts. Saddle blankets and packs need to be dry, and if you just packed in 15 miles they won't be. Lay them hair side up in the saddle pile or air them out over a pole before putting them away. They also make great sleeping pads and saves taking up room in your packs for air mattresses. Put your grain under the tarp or in the tent. Bridles, ropes and anything that can be dragged off, should be stored away. Deer just love to steal away with pack pads and bridles and chew them into little shreds. The deer isn't destructive by nature, he's just salt hungry and will ruin your new roping saddle by chewing the skirting right off it. Tarp on bottom and tarp on top, with a couple of good heavy rocks to keep the wind from blowing it up. Another common method is to cut some poles and make a saddle rack. Check the regulations for the area you are in to make sure this is okay. Keep in mind that if we want to enjoy it for years to come, the less we improve on the backcountry the better.

Roy Schwilke
Fallon, Nevada

Most elk hunters who pack in with horses or mules cause some environmental disturbance to trees and underbrush. Many even tie stock to trees or fashion a hitching post out of material at hand, and environmental destruction occurs. Here is a tip for no-impact backcountry horse tying. Use a high line between two trees and tie in "sliding eyes." These are made out of ¼-inch mild steel, and are available at tack stores and through outfitter supply catalogs. With tension off the lead rope, a sliding eye can be adjusted anywhere on the high line to suit your horses' needs. With tension on the lead rope (the horse pulling on it) friction keeps the sliding eye from moving.

Jerry Ponti
Otis Orchards, Washington

If hunting with horses, learn how to sling elk quarters on your riding saddle. Sling ropes and splitting hatchets can easily be carried in your saddle bags, and a walk to camp won't kill you. This can save a return trip back with packhorses to retrieve an elk, save your time, and allow more hunting or relaxing in camp. Be prepared to wash blood from your saddle upon reaching camp.

If using horses, do not leave your rifle in the horse's scabbard unattended. Many rifles have been damaged while hunters scouted, ate lunch, or returned to the cook tent for a cup of coffee. And don't leave your rifle leaning against the tree or hitch rack your horse is tied to—horseshoes don't do much for a riflestock's finish.

If packing elk antlers on horses, remember that every rack is different. Some fit best on the front quarters while others fit best on the hind quarters. To keep a medium-sized rack from poking the horse, tie a small, strong stick across the main beams near the fourth and fifth points. This stick will rest on the load and hold the rack up from the horse's rear.

If you are preparing for your first horseback elk hunt and have never ridden, find a stable at home and learn basic horsemanship. The more comfortable you are on a horse, the more rewarding your hunt of a lifetime may be. Don't be afraid to ask someone for help while learning to ride, most folks will be happy to help.

Tory Taylor
Dubois, Wyoming

If you have a horse or mule that is spooky around fallen game, here is a sure way to train them not to be. Snub them to a tree and place your coat over their eyes and tuck it into their halter so it doesn't fall off. Take some blood from the carcass and smear it all over their muzzle and in their nose. Then load the elk up and remove your coat. Everything will smell like elk blood to them. If you don't smear their nose with blood, when you remove your coat they will turn their head to smell what's on their back; when that happens, you usually have a rodeo on your hands.

Rick French
Wasilla, Alaska

If you're bringing in horses or mules from out-of-state, check with the proper authorities as to the health inspection and brand inspection of these animals. This is also true when you leave the state you've been hunting in.

Tom Morava
Rushville, Nebraska

- Watch your mount's ears. He will often hear, see and smell game before you.
- Let your stock drink at every opportunity. They get dehydrated, too.

- Your horse will leave you. Tie him high and secure. It's better to count ribs than tracks.
- When packing game, lead your stock in to the kill. Let them get used to the smell. Rub some blood on their nose. I have seldom had trouble loading meat after these precautions.

Richard E. Bennett
Big Fork, Montana

Much has been written about the "best" way to carry a rifle in a saddle scabbard. Let me suggest the one that works best for me. This is for a scoped, bolt action rifle. I mount my scabbard on the near (left) side, butt to rear, scope up. The angle of the scabbard is approximately 60 degrees. Although the bolt is toward the horse's rib cage, it will be against the skirts on some saddles. On my round-skirted saddle the bolt position is below the saddle skirt, but is "bridged" by the skirt and thus held away from the rib cage, and is further protected by a good hair saddle pad. I have never had a horse galled by the bolt. This position also puts the scope "right side up" which lessens weight on the scope and rubbing on the scope body. With anything other than a short, open-sighted saddle carbine, I do not care for a scabbard carried on the off (right) side. I feel that drawing a rifle from the left side while dismounting is not only awkward, but also unsafe. Of course, you sure don't want to dismount and run around your horse to grab your rifle! With the rifle on the near side, butt to rear, the rider can dismount and with the rifle at a shallow angle it can be easily drawn without any lift as would be necessary were the carry to be in the "butt up" position. Should the horse still be in any forward motion as the dismounted rider grabs the stock, such motion will naturally un-sheath the rifle. Everyone has their own way—but give this one a try!

Charles N. Pirtle
Las Cruces, New Mexico

Horses sometimes don't behave well, especially when they have been separated from their favorite buddy. Sometimes the ponies just go bonkers if they are tied up by themselves. So, to keep the cussing and the rodeo events to a minimum and to eliminate the whinnying from echoing across the entire mountainside, it is usually best to send riders out in pairs in the mornings. This is also a good safety measure so that in the event that something goes awry, you could have knowledge of where the hunter is, and get the necessary help.

Mark Cunningham
Crowley, Texas

CARING FOR MEAT AND TROPHY

To avoid spoiling the spoils of the hunt, keep an eye on the thermometer. Then again, you could always just pickle your bullets . . .

My pickup has a camper top on it to protect my hunting gear and "the cooler." The cooler is a 100-gallon galvanized water trough that measures 2 feet by 2 feet by 4 feet. I wrap it with 4 inches of fiberglass insulation, and place 2-inch ridged foam insulation on the bottom and 4 inches on the top. The fiberglass is wrapped with plastic and duct tape to keep the fiberglass away from the meat. A ¾-inch PVC pipe is attached to the drain plug and runs out to the tailgate. This keeps the water off the meat. The cooler is then covered with a heavy canvas tarp. It will hold two mule deer or one elk if they are quartered properly. With 80 pounds of ice, the meat will keep for three to five days, depending on the outside temperature.

Mark Hnatiuk
San Antonio, Texas

At the long distances at which I shoot my game, I have found it beneficial to soak my bullets in a concentrated salt solution, to prevent any meat from spoiling before I can reach my downed animal.

Jay D. Williams
Nampa, Idaho

Once you have your elk down and tagged, you might want to identify your trophy in case someone steals it. Write down how many points are on each antler, any identifying marks, etc. Take a close-up picture. Measure and record the length of each point, anything to help you prove that you're the rightful owner. I like to cut off a small piece of an ear, unless it's from an animal I want to get mounted. I pocket this puzzle piece of ear, and can produce it for a game warden if needed. Also, I sometimes tear a dollar bill in half, and cram half of it out of sight in the back of the animal's throat. I put the other half in my billfold. If someone steals my trophy, and is caught soon enough, I can produce my half of the dollar, and the game warden can reach down the throat of the animal and pull out the other half, and match up the serial numbers.

I also like to take a hardened steel bicycle lock cable and fasten the head and horns to my grill, or whatever I am hauling the head on when I drive home. And no, you do not want to haul the head and hide inside the rig, although some people might complain about seeing them on your vehicle's outside. If you put them inside where it is warm, all the fleas and ticks that are on them will jump off and the hide and head, and the inside of your vehicle will never be the same. Also, it will smell.

Harlan White
Canyonville, Oregon

Clean and quick field dressing method for elk and other big game animals: Slit skin back from tail to top of neck. Skin top side down to center line of stomach and down each leg to the knee and hock, then unjoint them there. Lift the shoulder by the freed knee end and, slicing between the ribs and shoulder, remove it. Lift the ham by the hock end and begin cutting very close along the pelvic bone until you reach the spine. Cut the meat away from the spine and remove the ham. Remove the backstrap. Remove neck meat, rib meat, and any other meat you can. Lay all these aside to cool. Lay the hide back over the carcass, turn the elk over and repeat the entire process on the other side. Now, take out two to four ribs over the heart and liver by unjointing them at each end and removing the heart and liver. The tenderloins can be reached by feeling in behind the innards and removing them from along the inner spine. This whole process is neat, clean, almost bloodless and very fast!

Joanne Bigman
Gold Hill, Oregon

If you can't get your elk out before dark, you can be sure the coyotes will have a feast before morning. We have left mule deer out overnight and come back in the morning to a pile of hair and bone chips and a few scraps of meat to mark the spot. If you can't hang the carcass out of reach of scavengers, it helps to hang a coat or handkerchief over the carcass on a stick. The best solution, though, is to leave a small transistor radio playing near the animal. (Not on a rap music station, though!)

On several occasions I have gone back to the kill with a tarp and sleeping bag, built a nice fire, and stayed right with the elk. They are such fine animals, they deserve the show of respect to put yourself out a bit to make sure you take good care of them.

Also, don't use those flimsy cheesecloth-type meat sacks. They will tear, stick to the meat, the yellowjackets will eat right through them, and they don't prevent flies from laying eggs on the meat. It's better to make your own out of heavier cloth, or go to the farmers' co-op and buy some big cotton sacks that sheep farmers pack wool in. They are cheap and make excellent meat sacks.

Harlan White
Canyonville, Oregon

This is a common scene that happens to elk hunters. You're a long way from camp, and in the last fading minutes of legal shooting light you knock an elk down. You just have a few basic items, such as your knife, saw, lunch, etc. You don't have any rope or game bags. On top of that you are probably chilled and really fatigued. To add insult to injury, the small flashlight you're holding in your teeth as you're field dressing your elk starts to fade out and slowly goes black. In this case you've got to do the best you can do. Roll the elk over on its back. Split the brisket and remove the esophagus. Place a stout stick in the rib cage to open it up and let the animal cool down. This is all common sense that most hunters practice regularly. But what most people don't realize is that the part of the elk that's touching the ground has no way of cooling. You've got two strikes against you. One, you still have the hide on, and two, you don't have any air flow to cool the part of the elk which is on the ground. The end result more times than not is tainted meat if the elk is left for long periods of time. I've talked to people who have done this and left their elk in 25-degree weather and six inches of snow. They figured the snow would cool the underside of the elk. This isn't true. The snow acts the same way as the bare ground, an insulator. The best thing to do in this case is to try and roll the elk over some and use logs to get it up off the ground. Even a little bit of air circulation under the elk will help a great deal.

In extremely frigid cold weather conditions there are a few tricks that will greatly increase your meat quality. First you have to know and understand the role rigor mortis plays in meat care. Most big game meat has about the same pH level. When you kill an animal, the meat goes through rigor mortis and the pH level drops. When this happens important proteins are released into the meat. It takes several hours for this to all happen. If the meat freezes before this process is finished, the process is stopped. Once the meat is thawed the process will not restart. The final result is, your meat will be elastic. It's like chewing on a piece of rubber. You should gut, skin and quarter your elk. Place the meat in good cotton game bags. Then lay them out on the ground, but don't stack the bags on top of one another. Cover the meat with the hide. Covering the hide with a tarp is an added bonus. Then pile snow on top of the tarp. These three layers act as insulators. If it's cold enough the meat will cool properly. Most importantly, the meat will not freeze. Let the meat set for several hours. Once the meat is properly cooled it's time to pack it out. The final result will be very tasty and chewable elk steaks.

Big game animals have a certain chemical balance in their muscles. They have energy in the form of oxygen and sugar. When they are stressed or run they burn up the energy quickly. Once burned up, lactic acid takes over, which messes up their chemical balance. If you don't give an animal time to relax, cool down, and regain its chemical balance, your meat will have a very gamy taste.

Another rule to live by in elk country is boning your meat. Don't do it! At least not right away. Granted, you and your buddies backpacked five miles and harvested an animal. Boning the meat will cut the weight of the packs and number of trips.

The drawback to doing this is that the muscles shrink and contract. If you don't believe me, the next time you harvest an animal and begin boning the meat, measure the backstrap. Then the next day measure it again, it will be a few inches shorter. It's best to leave as much meat on the bone as possible. Once the meat has contracted it gets a rubbery texture to it. You can try to tenderize it or even boil it, but it will not come back to it's original form. If you're going to bone your meat out anyway, it's better to do it after the meat has been hung and is completely cooled out.

Rick French
Wasilla, Alaska

When hunting in the late seasons (November), cold and especially wind chill can play havoc on fresh game meat. It is important that hung meat be allowed to freeze slowly. You want the meat to attain rigor mortis and then slowly relax. This usually takes anywhere from 10 to18 hours after death. If you don't allow this process to occur, your meat will forever be tough, regardless of what you do!

John McGannon
Daly City, California

Remove the hide from the carcass to allow for faster cooling. Removing the hide can drop the temperature of the carcass significantly. It may not always be practical to remove the hide from the carcass in the field, but it should be removed as soon as possible.

The ideal temperature to keep your meat at is below 40 degrees F (5 degrees C). This temperature inhibits the growth of most spoilage bacteria and molds.

Quarter the carcass to allow for faster cooling.

Wash the carcass with hot water to remove hair, dirt and debris. Wash both the inside and outside of the carcass.

Before gutting the animal, tie off the rectum with a shoestring or other suitable material. To do this, "bung" the rectum by cutting around the anus until it can be tied off. This will reduce the possibility of fecal contamination of your carcass.

Cut out all badly bruised and blood shot areas on the carcass, this meat is not edible and should not be processed with the rest of the carcass.

Inspect the following during field dressing of the carcass: liver, lungs, heart and lymph nodes. Look for discoloration, spots, swollen lymph nodes. Carefully inspect all injuries for gross infection or off odors.

Contact the local game meat processors before you go into the field, find out what services and facilities are available to you before you hunt. This will prevent you from wasting any of the hard earned meat.

Have the meat processed ASAP after the harvest. Most waste occurs due to neglecting the post-harvest carcass.

If your elk is to be processed by a meat cutter, ask/ answer the following: Will my meat be processed in a batch with other carcasses? What is the weight; bone in or out of the steaks and roasts? If having cooked or processed products (jerky, pepperoni, summer sausage, salami, German sausage, Polish sausage, etc.) made from your meat, what is the expected percentage return after processing, how is it to be packaged, in what sizes, and what percentage of fat is added to the ground meat?

Craig Doan
Troy, Idaho

Before removing entrails from your elk, your first step should be to remove the patch of belly hair that has usually been urinated on. Start above the anus and cut a wide half circle (about 12 inches) up the inside of one leg to mid-chest. Skin this flap and repeat for the other side. A separate knife should be used for this procedure. This will eliminate any contaminated hair from coming in contact with the meat.

Jim Alexy
Wembley, Alberta

If you harvest your elk way back in the boonies and it's warm outside, help is on its way but will take some time, then you need to cool the animal down. Carefully cut a slit on the top of the neck. Peel back the hide and cut open the meat on the thick upper neck. Prop it open with a stick. This allows the animal to cool down some even with the hide still on.

Jerry J. Farber
Saskatoon, Saskatchewan

To help remove the deadly "meat spoiling" heat from your freshly killed elk, skin the animal ASAP. Then remove the white sinew cord from the top of the neck. The heat will leave much faster with this cord removed. It runs from the top of the shoulder blades to the back of the head, all the way down the neck of the animal. I remove it on every animal my hunters down.

Al Marohn
Pickett, Wisconsin

In my field dressing kit I carry a pair of shoulder-length gloves that veterinarians use for doing pregnancy tests on horses and cattle. Over these I put on a pair of regular latex gloves and when I'm done dressing out my elk I take the gloves off, stuff them in a plastic bag and take them out of the woods to be disposed of properly.

Jeff Keller
Bend, Oregon

For cleaning big game, go to your local farm supply store and get veterinarian inspection gloves (shoulder-length vinyl glove). They will keep your hands and arms clean. If you keep the liver and heart, just pick it up in one hand and roll the glove off over the meat to keep it clean.

Mike R. Moore
Lincoln, Nebraska

A tip for the solitary hunter: I don't gut an elk, as it is unnecessary, messy and time-consuming, not counting the difficulty of doing it alone. I need to carry only a sharp knife, six game bags (the cheap ones do just fine) and some rope. I first position the animal on its side with the back downhill. I make a cut down the middle of the back from the tail to the back of the skull, then another from the back around the body to the tip of the breast bone. I then skin only one quarter at a time to keep it clean and reduce it to something I can handle. Next I remove it from the carcass by separating it at the joint with my knife, thereby doing away with the need for a saw or axe. As you remove the quarter, cover it with a game bag and attach a rope to hang it. When you finish with the front and rear quarters on the top side, remove the rest of the meat in one big chunk from the pelvis to the back of the skull and down the ribs to the sternum and put it in a game bag. Since you positioned the animal with the back downhill, it is easy to roll it over and do the same procedure to the other side. I am able to do the whole job from start to finish in a little over an hour by myself. All the meat is now ready to be hauled out as well as being kept clean and cooled quickly, a must for good table fare.

A tip for a one man operation is the making of a carrier that can handle elk. My requirements to make it are that it has to be light, easy to assemble in the field, strong, and most of all, cheap. I use a piece of ⅝-inch plywood cut to 16 by 32 inches for the base so it can be strapped to a backpack frame or fit into the pack itself. The wheel assembly I use has a pneumatic tire and comes from my wheelbarrow. It has a complete axle and mounting assembly that easily transfers from the wheelbarrow to the carrier. I made a horseshoe-shaped cut 5 inches wide and 12 inches long in one end of the plywood so the wheel will fit into the space with minimal clearance. To protect the wheel on top, I made a fender from two gallon-sized cans I obtained from a restaurant. I cut them about ¾ inches more than in half all the way from the top, down the side across the bottom and back up the other side. To get the needed clearance for the wheel, I added enough wood spacers on the top of the platform, then used screws to hold the cans in place over the wheel (this is the only permanently attached item on the platform). The wheel assembly is attached to the frame by bolts with wing nuts and lock washers. Handles are made from ¾-inch rigid conduit cut in about 7-foot lengths. They need to be long enough to go the entire length of the platform, bend up at about a 45-degree angle, then bend again at about waist height so it is parallel to the ground. I put wood dowels in the end that fits under the platform for reinforcement. I also put a "ram's horn" bend in the handle end to keep it from slipping out of my hands when going downhill. To help secure the handles to the platform, use two U-shaped brackets per side to hold it in line to the bottom of the platform and put two bolts per side with wing nuts through the platform and conduit to hold it all together.

This assembly can easily carry over half an elk with more being carried in the backpack used to ferry it up the mountain. When loading, place the most weight over the wheel so that you don't have to carry the weight with your arms. Remember to carry extra bolts and wing nuts as they can and will come out when you least expect it. My whole unit, including the backpack, weighs about 20 pounds and cost me, not including the wheel or backpack, under $15.

Richard Swedhin
Buena Vista, Colorado

How the meat is treated between the kill and when the elk is cut and wrapped determines how tender and how tasty your meat will be, and how your meat will smell when being cooked. I have found that getting the hide off as soon as possible and keeping all the dirt off the meat helps tremendously. When cutting meat, do not waste it, but keep in mind that unless it's red and tender, it won't taste any better in your hamburger than it will in your steak.

Trevor Yochum
Lewiston, Idaho

The next step after field dressing is to immediately skin the animal. A trick that we use in Arizona, because of our warmer temperatures, is to keep the meat cool by hanging it at night for proper chilling with complete air circulation. Then in the daytime, wrap the carcass in a tarp and put a bedroll around it and keep it in the shade. This will prevent spoilage in these warmer temperatures until you can leave camp to process the meat.

Pete Raubenheimer
Scottsdale, Arizona

When you have your elk hanging and the hide is off, there are always a few hairs left on it. Take a small butane torch and quickly go over the carcass. It will singe them right off and no one will say "Yuk! A hair!" at dinner time.

If you have to leave your animal or parts thereof, take off your T-shirt (which will best have your odor) and leave it on the carcass. Coyotes won't bother it.

Rick Seymour
Glenwood Springs, Colorado

Here is a make-do-in-a-pinch packer's frame: Leave the hide on one front quarter. Make two cuts in the hide about 2 inches apart and 16 to 18 inches long. Separate the hide from the meat to form a strap. Make a duplicate strap to form the straps of a pack frame. Put it on your back and head for camp.

Daniel Manial
Holly, Michigan

If you want the best possible meat, get the hide off as soon as possible even if you have to do it in the field. They can be skinned and quartered on the ground. If you have to pack it out, bone it out and put the meat in sacks. Use an old type handsaw to split elk. The saw teeth are six to an inch, and it works best for me. Anyone can pull up an elk with a three-wheel block and tackle. If you can afford an electric winch, go for it.

When you have an elk hanging in camp and are bothered with flies, use pepper. It doesn't hurt the meat and the flies don't like it. I don't bother with game bags or sacks anymore. Old bed sheets work just fine. For the trip home, use your bedroll on the bottom with a large open tarp on this, bed sheets next, and the meat on this. Fold sheets up onto the meat, placing a last sheet on top to cover and keep meat clean. Fold the rest of the tarp up and over the sheets, and finally, cover this with the rest of your canvas tarps. Never use plastic to cover meat. Don't waste any of the meat. The tongue, heart and liver are the finest.

Jack Lutch
Wickenburg, Arizona

Hunters should carry a small container of pepper with them on the hunt. If you get an animal down in the late evening, and are unable to get it out of the area that day, all you need to do is sprinkle the pepper generously over the entire carcass. The pepper repels most animals and they will generally leave the meat and carcass alone. The pepper will not affect the taste of the meat.

After you have your game on a meat pole, I would recommend covering your animal with a large sheet of untreated white canvas after skinning. The canvas reflects the sunlight, helping to keep the meat cool, and also repels the snow and rain to keep the meat dry. The canvas keeps the animal clean when hanging and transporting. The canvas can be found at most outfitting supply stores.

If you shoot a nice animal and want a shoulder mount, don't cut the throat.

When gutting an elk, it makes the job a lot easier if you split the brisket with a small saw after you have opened the stomach area. From there on out, gutting the animal will be a lot easier.

Adam Bowers
Gypsum, Colorado

CO

This tip is useful to those that quarter their game in the field. After shooting an animal, skin it entirely, then roll it onto its stomach. Remove the backstraps, then roll it onto its back again. Remove both front shoulders, neck meat and the hindquarters. This leaves a nice neat package of internal organs still intact within the rib cage. Remove the liver, then move the rest of the internal organs out of the way to expose the tenderloins. This process is very quick and efficient.

Dean Hendrickson
Palmdale, California

CO

A dead elk is a lot bigger than a dead deer and can be awkward to field dress by yourself. I pack along several lengths of sash cord or heavy twine, which I use to tie the elk's legs to brush, logs, stones or whatever is handy, in order to keep the animal in a spread-eagle position while I work on it.

If your plan is to cut the animal up for transportation, consider an alternative to the traditional process of field dressing. Begin by laying the animal on its side and splitting the hide down the center of the back and down the center of the belly. Remove the hide from the upper side of the animal. Cut off the backstrap, ham, shoulder, flank, brisket, neck and meat from between the ribs, the same as you would if the carcass were skinned and hung up. Turn the animal over and repeat the process on the other side. At this time, the tenderloins, liver, heart, kidneys, etc., can be harvested. The two sides of the hide can still be tanned into leather.

Ben H. Wolcott
Milton, FL

In order to make boning your elk in the field easier and to keep the meat clean, bring along a clean, new piece of corrugated carton, approximately 2 by 3 feet. This provides a great, non-slip, clean way to bone out meat. One rancher was so impressed with the care I took and the method I used that he said I could hunt on his place every year.

Randall Tlachac
Plymouth, Minnesota

Always have several good, sharp knives in your daypack. Gutting and cutting will quickly dull a knife. And if archery hunting you don't want to stop and sharpen a knife while the flies get to the meat.

L. Minish
Highlands Ranch, Colorado

Carry a diamond steel in your backpack. Make four or five cuts and hit the steel two or three times. One knife will then do the entire job with ease.

Rick Seymour
Glenwood Springs, Colorado

You've hunted hard, the shot was true and the elk is down. Now what? To efficiently dress that elk, a sharp knife is needed. Here is how to sharpen your knife: Use a double grit stone (coarse on one side, and medium on the other) about 6 inches long. Start coarse, using a few drops of cooking oil on the stone to float away the loose grit and bits of steel that accumulate as you sharpen and tend to clog the pores in the stone. Raise the blade to contact the stone and draw the blade across the stone, sliding it the length of the stone, six strokes. Turn the blade away for six strokes. Work from the heel of the blade to the tip of the blade, and hold your angle. Switch to the medium stone and repeat. It's that easy. Use a folding saw to open the brisket and quarter the elk. Save your knife blade to cut hide and meat!

John R. Harvieux
Balsam Lake, Wisconsin

After skinning the animal on a warm weather hunt, sprinkle black pepper on the meat to protect it from flies and other insects before putting it in a game bag or when you don't have a game bag available. The pepper does not affect the taste of the meat since the crust that forms is trimmed away when the meat is processed. This also works on the capes and skins before you get to the taxidermist.

Barney Hammond
Calhan, Colorado

No need to rush from camp to a locker plant with that elk carcass. Use the old time method for meat care without refrigeration. Skin elk as soon as possible. Bone meat. This reduces weight and gets rid of the heat holding properties of bone. Lay meat on a "ladder-like" rack of dry poles or tree limbs laid on the ground to let air circulate and keep meat from contact with wet/dirty ground conditions. This is preferable in a shady spot, but not necessary in cold, sunny conditions. Meat can be left on this rack or hung and chilled through the night. It should be bagged in cloth bags once glazed. Before the morning sun gets on the meat, it should be wrapped in a large tarp (preferably canvas) and kept in shade—moving it as necessary, until sundown. The meat is then uncovered to be again exposed to the cold night air. Always avoid stacking meat before it is cooled, and make sure it is protected from rain. This is the place to use your plastic tarp—either as a fly which lets air circulate, or directly on top of the trapped meat during the daytime hours. Meat can be kept in this manner for a week or 10 days even with very warm daytime temperatures and much longer if temperatures are fairly cold.

Although many new elk hunters are unaware of the ivories found in both bulls and cows, most elk hunters I know are intrigued by and collect these pleasing mementos of the hunt. Instead of just throwing them in a box or drawer, they should be used and enjoyed. Much elk ivory jewelry is shown in *Bugle* magazine. Less expensive uses include key rings, holster and knife thongs, and one of my favorites, as "pulls" on the strings of ceiling fans/light fixtures.

Charles N. Pirtle
Las Cruces, New Mexico

I trained my Newfoundland dog to pull a sled. He helps me pack out game when there is a sufficient amount of snow on the ground. The dog wears a special weight-pulling harness attached to a custom-made sled and follows me as I pull my sled. He can easily pull a hind quarter of elk through less than 18 inches of dry snow. I use a dog pack on him when there is no snow and fill it with boned meat.

Dan Trochta
West Yellowstone, Montana

Here is a tip for getting your elk back to camp or your vehicle after it has fallen. We found the task was made much easier with the use of a calf sled. A calf sled is a type of plastic sled used to haul new-born calves to shelter if they are born out in the elements. We simply split the elk in two and drag out the halves. If no hunting buddies are available for assistance, the elk could be boned out and the whole thing could easily be drug out by a single hunter. A wooden toboggan could also be used, but the calf sled makes things easier because it has sides on it to keep the critter from falling off the sled. Of course it is easier to pull if there is snow on the ground, but it also pulls fairly well over grass. The sleds can be obtained at any farm and ranch supply store.

John A. Paczkowski
Bismarck, North Dakota

This tip is for all those hardy elk hunters whose second most important piece of gear, next to their hiking boots, is their pack frame. The next time you have to pack out an elk on your back, try using black bungee cords to strap a quarter to your pack frame. I use the thick black ones that you can purchase at the auto parts store. Buy a couple of 24-inch-long straps and prepare to become attached to your elk. You can pull these straps guitar string tight and they will hold no matter how many hills you fall down. Place a quarter of elk on your pack frame and crisscross the bungee cords as many times and as tightly as you can. It actually takes longer to explain than to actually do. Your partner will still be tying his first granny knot and you will be on your way down the trail. Bungee cords are cheap, strong, lightweight and quick to use, will not loosen and will not allow your load to shift while you are negotiating gnarly blowdown or steep terrain. No more frozen rope knots or stopping to retie your floppy load. Just pure confidence that you are one with your elk quarter all the way to the truck.

Bill Hanlon
Sparwood, British Columbia

Many hunters have to leave their trophy in the hills overnight and coyotes get into it. To solve that problem I have found that if you leave a few empty cartridges in its chest cavity the coyotes stay away. The smell of humans and gunpowder makes them nervous.

Shad Butikofer
Blackfoot, Idaho

To quarter an elk, many hunters use a saw or axe. I prefer two single-blade hatchets of medium weight. Use one to drive the other through bone. The two hatchet splitting method is easier than a saw and more accurate than a single axe.

An army surplus military stretcher and a buddy can make carrying elk quarters to your vehicle an easier job. In a solo situation, a heavy-duty wheel-barrow often beats a backpack frame.

Meat cutting businesses normally add up to 25 per-cent beef fat to elk meat ground into hamburger. If you want to eat beef, eat beef. If you want to eat elk, leave the beef and pork fat out of your elk trim. I have my elk trim ground with no fat added. This pure ground elk hamburger makes tasty patties, stew meat, meat loaf, jerky, burritos, enchiladas, spaghetti meatballs, and breakfast sausage. And my arteries are happier.

Tory Taylor
Dubois, Wyoming

Elk meat can be transported long distances and aged by deboning, placed on block ice in coolers and cov-ered with crushed ice for five or more days. The meat can then be processed into choice cuts and frozen.

An elk hide can be salted with three to five pounds of salt for several days, drained and resalted, rolled hair side out and shipped to a tanning shop for processing into a beautiful rug.

A very inexpensive trophy mount can be made using the European style sawing behind the antlers, eye sockets and nose. Remove all flesh; after drying, paint skull with a flat white.

If you find yourself alone with an elk down and no rope, you can lock a hind leg behind the bull's antlers to help reach the stomach and chest area.

Jack Yates
Hazlehurst, Mississippi

Take your own quarter-meat bags even on outfitted hunts. It helps keep track of your own meat and capes. Bone and trim aggressively for great results at the table.

When caping for shoulder mounts, cut clear back to the middle of the animal in order for the taxidermist to have enough hide to work with.

Richard E. Bennett
Bigfork, Montana

When on hunts many road miles away, or when I'm not in a hurry to get home, and I have meat that has been processed and frozen, I carry a small freezer in my pickup and a long extension cord. While overnighting at a motel or campground with facilities, I plug in and never worry about thawed meat.

Double wrap your meat for long-term storage.

Thomas J. Frey
Las Vegas, Nevada

OUTFITTERS AND GUIDES

Hunting up a good guided hunt, and making the most of it, is a skill and a challenge in itself. Equip yourself with the knowledge and advice of people who've been there.

Many of us get to take "dream" hunts just once in a lifetime. Sometimes we manage to set aside funds for a couple of trips. In an attempt to save money, we may take shortcuts which result in less than pleasant journeys. So carefully consider each decision you make in purchasing equipment, planning accommodations, and hiring an outfitter.

Questions to avoid when first consulting an outfitter are "How much?" and "What's your success rate?" These show that you are just window shopping and don't understand a lot. Start with "Tell me about your hunts." This will give the outfitter a chance to tell you the things he thinks are important.

Other good questions to ask an outfitter are: What are the various types of hunts you offer? How many hunters will be in camp? Will I be responsible for any food or supplies? Will I be sleeping in a cabin or in a tent? What's the weather usually like during the hunt? Can you promise me an opportunity to shoot an animal? (When I hear someone guarantee 100 percent success, I walk away. There are too many variables in a real hunt to ever guarantee that I will fill my tag.)

Remember you're buying a service, not an animal.

Your equipment has to be familiar to you. Practice makes perfect. Don't wait until a week before the hunt to start shooting. Your body and mind are going to have plenty of other problems, don't add another.

Kraig Kaatz
Oak Forest, Illinois

Most hunting guides have a thorough understanding of their craft, an intimate knowledge of their quarry and its habitat, high moral standards and impeccable taste. They are also sensitive, and easily injured by a breech of manners. Observe these rules while on a guided hunt:

1. Never put a live round in the chamber until the guide tells you to.
2. Never demonstrate that your safety is on by pulling the trigger.
3. Don't tie up your horse, let the guide do it.

It will still get untied and wander off, but the guide won't be able to blame you.

4. Never ask, "Which way to camp?" Philosophical questions like this can confuse the guide and disrupt his train of thought. Also, don't ask "How much farther?" It forces your guide to lie. Do not accuse your guide of being lost. He knows where he is; it's usually camp that is lost.

5. If placed on a stand, do not go looking for the guide, thinking he might be lost.

6. Do not shoot the universal three-shot help signal just because you are lonesome.

7. Do not shoot the universal three-shot help signal if you are bow hunting.

8. Do not ask the guide if you can rest the gun barrel on his shoulder to steady your shot.

9. Do not giggle when your guide blows his elk bugle.

10. Do not ask the guide to return to camp to get your forgotten lunch, or return to the lunch spot to get your forgotten rifle.

If you've never hunted elk, especially with a bow, go with someone who has.

Bill Sansom
St. Regis, Montana

You can gain a wealth of information by frequenting gun shows, sports shows, outdoor expos, etc. Outfitters and guides from many parts of the country will have booths at these shows. In talking to these people face-to-face, you can get info that you won't get from their ads or while speaking to them on the phone.

Thomas J. Frey
Las Vegas, Nevada

HUNTING SAFE AND SMART

How to avoid discomfort, disaster and death.

One of the most important things you can do for elk hunting success is to be in good physical condition, especially if you're a flatlander like I am. You can't harvest an elk when you're always looking for a place to take a breather. (Also, knowing the area in advance is a major factor in your chances of success.)

Scott Johnson
St. Francis, Minnesota

Hunting in the mountains can be strenuous, even for someone who has been training hard at lower elevations. Climbing into the high country is best accomplished by using logging roads or other paths. Hunt your way back down through the dark timber.

Vern Humphrey
Seaford, Virginia

During several hunts over the years, I've seen the following subtle but extremely dangerous mistake: After the excitement of bagging your elk, the work begins; one or more people are intently working back and forth over the carcass, and nobody remembers that the hunter chambered a second round as they approached the animal. A rifle lays near, bullet in the chamber, safety off. Disaster awaits. Please, everybody, secure all firearms before tending to your animal.

Require everyone you hunt with to verify that their guns are empty before loading or entering the vehicle. In 30+ years of hunting, I've never seen a responsible hunter take offense to this practice. A high school classmate of mine was lost because this wasn't done.

Chris Sandmark
Casper, Wyoming

Unload your gun when it gets dark! While I was guiding one of the things that scared me most was a hunter walking around in the dark with a shell in the chamber and the safety off. More than once, even after I had asked them to unload their guns, I was blinded by a muzzle blast in the dark after a hunter stumbled or fell.

Barnery Hammond
Calhan, Colorado

When elk hunting, always be alert for another hunter moving in and shooting at the same vocal bull as you. This could spell danger if either hunter is not aware of the other's presence.

Reginald Brooks
Saskatoon, Saskatchewan

Don't use your rifle scope to glass game, movement or even distant country. It's an accident waiting to happen. I've had people glass me with their rifle scope while sitting on top my horse. It takes the fun right out of hunting, and it's not safe at all.

When you approach a downed elk, do it from the uphill rear side. If it's a steep hillside and the elk is hung up against a tree, it is real easy to get kicked or hooked with a horn from the downhill side. Worse yet, all the elk has to do is move a little and it may come dislodged from the tree and it will go rolling down the mountain. You could very easily have a several hundred pound elk rolling right over the top of you.

When you knock an elk down on a mountainside, get about 50 to70 yards above it. Then approach it from the rear. A wounded or scared animal will often try to escape danger by running uphill. If the elk regains its feet and flees uphill you can usually make it sidehill or go downhill. In either case you may get a couple extra shots off if need be. If you approach from downhill the elk may see you and run.

Sometimes you won't even get a chance to shoot when approaching from downhill.

Rick French
Wasilla, Alaska

I carry a day pack in the field, filled with all I need for comfort and survival should something go awry. Along with all the basics, I also carry a couple of yellow or green Cyalume light sticks. They are not much larger than a writing pen and bright enough to read by. They glow brightly for up to 12 hours. In Alaska, I hung one in my tent at night allowing me to see anything I might need, quickly.

On several occasions, I have left field dressed animals unattended overnight. More than once, I have seen coyotes in the immediate area and/or fresh bear sign. After field dressing, I remove my outer shirt and place it on a nearby bush or tree limb, I also attach a "light stick" to a nearby bush or if necessary, to the animal's hoof. Lastly, I urinate a few yards from the animal. Any one of these practices might be enough, but the combination of all three has always worked for me.

In total darkness, I have been able to see the "glow" from a mile away or more. I purchase "light sticks" at a local army surplus store, but have seen them available mail order. Price varies from approximately $5 to $10 a dozen.

Allan Myers
Texico, New Mexico

Climbing hills or stairs builds quadriceps. Use a treadmill on a steep angle.

When ascending a slope, keep your hands above your waist. Lean into a steep uphill slope or keep your body vertical. Lean back slightly going down steep slopes. Place your hands on your hips when hiking, insert thumbs into sternum strap to increase circulation, pick up bottom of the pack with your arms to rest your shoulders often. Cross fast water with a stick/staff planting it upstream and unbuckle your waist belt in case you need to shed your pack. Powder your feet and place a strip of adhesive tape or moleskin on your heel before a hike. Change socks often.

Use a flashlight even on bright nights, due to ledges, holes, etc., to prevent falls. Use a red filter on your flashlight.

Mike Zimmermann
Houston, Texas

A camouflaged bandanna is a versatile article of clothing to have. Tie it loosely around your neck and pull it up over your nose to conceal your face during close elk encounters. When it is hot out, soak it in water and drape it over your neck to cool you down. A bandanna also makes a good bandage, helps keep your face warm on cold days, protects your neck from sunburn, and is a good dust filter when riding an ATV.

Todd Corsetti
Pocatello, Idaho

Maintaining warmth is important when elk hunting because the seasons are typically in the colder months. Layering of clothing has long been talked about and certainly has its merits. There are other, much easier methods to control ventilation when climbing or otherwise exerting yourself. It always helps to remove your hat. Heat travels up your body like a chimney, and removing your hat allows the heat to dissipate on out of your furnace, as it were. Unbutton your shirt a few buttons at the top, or clear to the waist if necessary. Then unbutton your shirtsleeves and roll them up to allow ventilation. Gloves should come off right away, too. When you have achieved the elevation or vantage point you desire, then close up these vents. First, put your hat back on, close up your shirt, sleeves and front buttons. Button the top collar button to seal up the space around your neck.

Another easy tip for controlling body heat is to wear a skiing-type head band. The head band may be used for the ears if desired, although you should keep the band just over the tops of the ears so as not to muffle sounds. A headband can also be pulled down around your neck like a turtleneck. With two headbands, you can keep both your neck and your ears warm. Ear bands can easily be removed and stowed in a pocket when climbing.

Dick Taylor
Oregon City, Oregon

A quick uplifting source of energy is tea with honey, either hot or cold. This is a double barrel blast. The sugar in honey is quickly metabolized, providing a sugar jolt; the second barrel, lagging shortly behind, comes from the caffeine in the tea. This concoction really works!

Dan Nelson
Mesa, Arizona

Dehydration is the silent killer. Physical fatigue is generally due to dehydration, not hunger. Drink 5 to 6 quarts of water per day. Ten percent dehydration causes a 30- to 40-percent decrease in your body's heating ability. Do not eat snow; instead, add snow to a half-full canteen to melt it.

Mike Zimmermann
Houston, Texas

One of the necessities of a tough hunt is adequate water or liquids. I have tried canteens and cans, both of which are noisy and bulky. I have been using a foil-pouch drink as a great way to carry and fill the need for liquids. The foil pouches are quiet, convenient, and come with a drinking straw. Once you drink the juice, the foil pouch can be crushed and discarded back at camp. I've started keeping several in my backpacks and truck, using them for sporting events and deer, turkey and elk hunting.

Jere L. Yates
Bartlett, Tennessee

I always take two pair of well broken-in boots, two years old or older, on my elk hunts, to ensure I won't have blisters.

Jack Yates
Hazlehurst, Massachusetts

Use one-day disposable contacts. No daily cleaning with dirty hands.

L. Minish
Highlands Ranch, Colorado

Carry a disposable camera.

Be courteous to that other hunter—you may harvest an animal and need his help if/when he comes back through.

Rick Seymour
Glenwood Springs, Colorado

A good tree step system can be built by purchasing some black PVC 2½-inch pipe. Cut the PVC pipe into 6-inch pieces with 45 degree angles cut on either end. Next, drill a ½-inch hole through the middle of the pipe. Purchase some good quality 1-inch webbing and metal buckles. Feed the webbing through the ½-inch hole and around the tree and use the pipe as a step. Several can be made and carried in a pack. They are very lightweight and will not damage trees.

A compact camera tripod for bow hunters can be made of a 3-by-2-inch block of oak or similar material. Drill holes up into the bottom of the block on angles and tightly insert your correct size of field or target point up into the hole, leaving the threaded end exposed. Next obtain a piece of threaded material the correct size to fit your camera base and epoxy this into the top of the block. When you are ready to take your field picture, simply pull out your block and screw on three arrows for legs, screw on your camera body, and shoot your best field picture ever!

Reginald Brooks
Saskatoon, Saskatchewan

A shooting stick can have many more uses than just shooting. I have found it to be so useful that I never go hunting anymore without taking it along. My design consists of a 34-inch long piece of $^5/_{16}$-inch dowel with a 4-inch piece of dowel across the top. The top piece should be notched to allow it to fit flat against the top of the vertical piece. Predrill the top piece along with the 34-inch vertical piece and paint the whole thing flat black. I also drill out the vertical piece and install two ¼-inch pieces of dowel at an angle about 4 inches and 8 inches below the top piece to form a groove to allow your barrel to rest in. These only need to be about an inch long. This gives you a total of three positions to rest your gun on when shooting. This shooting stick makes a great walking stick, but what I have found most useful is for glassing. I spend long hours glassing and have found that resting the glasses on top of this stick is a great help! I originally made this stick for use when varmint calling, but now use it every time I go out. I've also found it very useful hunting for javelina in Arizona when trying to move thorny brush out of your way.

Dean Hendrickson
Palmdale, California

To beef up things that must endure a lot of stress, like shoulder straps on hunting packs and buttons on heavy, bulky coats, try re-sewing the items with dental floss. I've had years of service out of things by switching from thread to floss. It works!

Les Smith
Grand Junction, Colorado

Since it's almost impossible to sit still when it's well below freezing, I invented this system. I put alcohol in a metal imitation candle (with wick). I bury the candle to ground level and put a wire coil above it to keep anything away from flame. With a poncho over me, it makes a mini hot house, and I can sit for hours down to zero degrees. The candles are from restaurant supply. They use lamp oil, but I found it smudged my clothes and smelled. Alcohol is the cleanest burning fuel and makes the hottest flame!

Dead-eye Dodson
North Hills, California

If you can't whistle, and you don't happen to have a store-bought whistle with you, use a spent cartridge casing. Blow over the top of it until you get a high-pitched whistle that is louder than what most people can do with their mouths. This will let companions know where you are and you can also send signals to fellow hunters. (The expired cartridge cannot have any cracks in it. If it does, it will not make a sound.)

Brad Chandler
Rice Lake, Wisconsin

To keep your boot laces from coming untied or getting caught on brush, get a pair of cord locks like those on stuff sacks. Slip them over your laces, pull your laces tight then snug up the lock to keep tight. Your shoes will never come untied again. Cut off the excess laces. Make sure the laces are long enough to let you get your boot off without taking the lock completely off the lace. Usually leaving the lace about long enough to touch the sole is about right. Singe the ends of the laces or use superglue to keep them from unraveling.

Mike Moore
Lincoln, Nebraska

When hunting in big country, consider taking a handheld GPS unit, along with your map and compass. The prices for these units are reasonable, they're lightweight, and can be a real life saver. Read the instructions and learn how to use your GPS before elk season starts so you'll be confident in its use. Buy a good map of the area you're going to hunt and mark the borders using a special latitude/longitude ruler you can buy at a local map store. When you leave camp or your vehicle in the morning turn on your GPS and log your starting point. As you travel about on your hunt, periodically record significant landmarks along your route as way points. You can also mark the location of downed game. That way you can always find your way back to camp after a long hard day of chasing elk. You'll also find that by methodically observing and recording your way points you'll be much less likely to get lost in the first place.

Mike Sanders
Spokane, Washington

You can hunt safe and smart by always making it a habit of carrying not one, but two compasses with you.

Reginald Brooks
Saskatoon, Saskatchewan

I have enjoyed the ease of a bubble compass pinned to my vest or outer hunting garment. I can quickly glance down at it and know the direction I need to head. Wherever I'm facing is the direction the compass reads. I also own a larger compass which takes time to open and to settle down. The bubble compass is quick and easy.

Dick Taylor
Oregon City, Oregon

I always wear a small pin-on ball compass that I can quickly glance down at to get my bearings. When hunting a thick stand of lodgepole it will keep you on track.

An MRE (meal ready-to-eat) is a great thing to have in your backpack if you have to spend the night out in the woods. Heat up a little water and boil the bag in it and you have a hot meal complete with crackers and cheese, dessert and a towlette to clean up with after you've eaten. (Some MREs are heated up chemically by just adding cold water to a special pouch and placing the main entree packet inside it.)

Jeff Keller
Bend, Oregon

Carry in your pocket or pack several zip-locked bags, pencil and orange post-it notes. These come in handy when you are to meet a partner at a predetermined spot. If you need to leave before they arrive, write a note, seal it and hang it on a branch or rock. The orange will stand out for easier visibility. Make sure your partners are aware of this so they can keep an eye out for it.

Tim Sattler
Yakima, Washington

If planning to meet another hunter at a particular time or place, confirm it several times. If possible, mark the location on a map and write the information down. Repeat the rendezvous point to each other to make sure each party understands. Valuable time or even a life could be at stake.

Before leaving camp or splitting up, check with your hunting partners about necessities. Do you have water? Compass? Fire starting material? Cartridges? Etc?

When going into an unfamiliar area, stop and look behind you occasionally. Mention useful landmarks to your companions, such as the tree limb that looks like an elephant's trunk or the peak that appears like a bald man with a beard and no teeth. It is not advisable to use clouds as landmarks!

If you are using your vehicle every day to get to your hunting area, keep it topped off with fuel. Your vehicle could be your home until help arrives.

When seeing another hunter in the wild, acknowledge him with a wave. That way you are both aware of each other's presence.

Butch Grusing
Fountain, Colorado

I know it is not easy to take your knife or an angle-head grinder to your new pair of $200 boots, but by making the tread a bit unusual, altering the tread cleats somehow to make them very individual, you can instantly identify your tracks. Get your hunting partners to do the same. Then you will know who it was that crossed through your hunting area, or if that track you saw was a stranger's. By the time a hunt is over, I have usually sabotaged my hunting partners' treads enough that I can tell them all apart. It makes your hunt more interesting, and can be life-saving if anyone gets lost. You can tell searchers exactly what track to look for and follow. It's helpful to sketch the treads of everybody's boots and keep the sketches with you, to help you remember whose are whose, and where the special markings are.

Harlan White
Canyonville, Oregon

While hunting, stop often to look back, monitor vertical and horizontal distances, keep track of time so you know how long it takes to get somewhere and to return, watch the sun. Use a compass and altimeter.

Tell your hunting companions you are prepared to spend the night in the woods so they don't worry or search unnecessarily. Leave a map with someone, with the general area you're hunting circled. Give them an estimated return date.

Carry chemical light sticks.

If you're hunting and there's lightning, stay off peaks and ridges, away from large trees, boulders, etc.

If you become lost, stay put. Decide you want to live. Admit you are lost. Remember to STOP (Sit, Think, Observe, Plan).

Survival kit—rain pants, wool gloves, wool hat/ scarf, wool socks, metal cup to boil water, multitool knife, mini flashlight (extra batteries and bulbs), waterproof matches or lighter, candles/firestarters, space blanket, compass and map, whistle, signal mirror, aerial flares, chemical light sticks, notepad/pen, food, field first-aid kit, water purification tablets, spare prescription medicine and glasses, toilet paper, heavyweight extra large plastic garbage bags, 100 feet of small nylon cord, picture of family, aluminum foil, safety pins, saw, etc.

Mike Zimmermann
Houston, Texas

Go nowhere without your day pack. It should contain survival items—flashlight, gloves, socks, food, fire-starters, first-aid kit, compass, maps and rain gear.

Richard E. Bennett
Bigfork, Montana

I never leave camp for elk hunting without a small, orange day pack for both convenience and safety. The contents of my pack include waterproof matches, fire starter, parachute cord, trail flagging, map of the area (if in unfamiliar terrain), compass, poncho, space blanket, folding bone saw, plastic military surplus canteen, can of beans and wieners or Vienna sausage, individual container of pudding, single serving of fruit cocktail, apple, and a spoon. This small and, except for the water, light accompaniment provides your needs for a day-long hunt, and if something unexpected happens, may save your life.

Grady E. McCright
Las Cruces, New Mexico

A camouflaged poncho combined with waterproof gaiters is ideal, lightweight and inexpensive rain gear. The poncho can also be used as a bivouac, as a ground cloth for cleaning an animal, and as a temporary blind.

When elk hunting, take enough gear so that you could safely stay in the woods overnight if required. The following items can easily fit in a small fanny pack for elk hunting:

Flashlight with extra batteries and bulb
Waterproof matches, lighter and fire starter
Surveyor's tape
Knife, bone saw and Leatherman tool
Your license and tags
Toilet Paper
Rain poncho
Food and water for one full day and night
A few iodine pills for water treatment
Wind checker
Thin nylon rope
Compass
Emergency blanket

Todd Corsetti
Pocatello, Idaho

Carry a backpack with everything you will need to hunt all day and field dress an elk. Include first-aid supplies, survival gear, knives, saw, flashlight, water, rope, lunch and meat bags.

Get in the best shape you can. Walk, hike, or run.

Use boots that are used, not new.

Layer your clothing so you can adjust to changing weather conditions.

Keep dry and drink lots of water.

Mike Mobbs
Olympia, Washington

Hypothermia prevention: drink fluids and eat lots of carbohydrates (pasta, bread, potatoes, etc.); dress in layers; cover head and neck; keep coat cinched tightly around waist; practice making fires in the worst conditions.

Mike Zimmermann
Houston, Texas

Most hunters, hikers and outdoorsmen carry just one waterproof matchcase. I carry several—in my pack, pants pocket, and in each jacket and vest. That way I never "forget" my matches.

Matches left in an airtight case for an extended period often become useless. When struck, they smoke and sputter, but most fail to ignite. Thus, fresh matches should be installed in your matchcase each season.

The old standby "strike anywhere" or "kitchen" matches have virtually been replaced by "strike on box" only matches. These are useless in your matchcase, or anywhere, without the box. Beware what you buy, as they look identical!

Charles N. Pirtle
Las Cruces, New Mexico

Take an egg carton, and put one or two cotton balls in each hole. Put newspaper under egg carton in case of spillage. Melt wax and pour over the cotton and let cool. Cut carton into individual firestarter cups. Works every time, even in the rain. Just add small twigs and light with a match.

Homer Atwood, Jr.
Milwaukie, OR

All elk country can and often does experience rapid and unexpected changes in the weather during hunting season. A hunter may encounter high winds, rain, sleet, snow, and possible bitter cold. For over twenty years, I have carried a simple, cheap, yet effective fire starter to kindle wet tinder for warmth or just to heat a can of beans and wieners. Take a spent shotgun shell of any caliber, place a cotton wick all the way from the open end to the primer and fill the cavity with melted paraffin. In a few minutes you have a durable candle fit for the pack or pocket. The fabrication is simpler if you tie an overhand knot in the bottom end of the string and dip it in the melted paraffin before inserting the solidified wick in the empty shell. I make several at a time and keep one alongside each waterproof container of matches in numerous places. The entire plastic shell will be consumed and the only residue that requires packing out is the brass rim of the devoured case.

Grady E. McCright
Las Cruces, New Mexico

Place clothes dryer lint balls in a paper egg carton (not plastic, it melts). Drizzle melted paraffin onto each lint ball. Once cool, double zip-locked bag a few and throw in your fanny pack. Depending upon the amount of wax, one ball should last five minutes or longer. The lint is important in that it can be ignited with a steel flint, which will spark even if wet. If you don't have time to melt paraffin, petroleum jelly worked into the lint (or cotton balls) will also work, but usually only lasts 3 to 5 minutes.

Robert Main
Coquille, Oregon

For a cheap fire starter, take a rinsed tuna can, cut a strip of cardboard the depth of the can, and roll it up until it fills the can. Then pour melted wax into the can until filled. To use, gouge the cardboard a little to make a small wick, then light.

Mike Moore
Lincoln, Nebraska

A small plastic bottle with a screw-on cap filled with cotton balls which have been soaked with rubbing alcohol serve two purposes. First, the cotton balls can be used to treat a small cut or wound, and second, even in a strong wind or snowstorm, the cotton balls and container can be lit with a single match, making it possible to start a large fire. The bottle with cotton balls inside will provide a large flame for at least ten minutes or so.

A good firestarter to carry is dryer lint. It weighs nothing and if placed in a little zip-locked bag can be in your pack always for the one time you may need an emergency firestarter.

Al Marohn
Pickett, Wisconsin

I call this personal invention a lifesaver: Pour the contents of a bottle of Cutex clear nail polish into an empty 35 mm film canister, then mix in as much 4831 rifle powder as can be incorporated. Cut off the little plastic brush from the fingernail polish applicator and stick it into the mixture for a wick to light it. Let it set up hard, with the lid off. Then you have a firestarter that can hardly be put out once it is lit.

Harlan White
Canyonville, Oregon

A sandwich bag with a good wad of pine pitch in it will start a fire in a downpour. I've used it and it works.

Jeff Keller
Bend, Oregon

The best firestarter is a cotton ball with a little petroleum jelly. It's perfect for campfires and cook stoves, and it's cheap!

Tom Beaton
Coeur D'Alene, Idaho

Every year I would leave something at home. What I needed was a list. A master list. So, after returning home after my yearly elk hunt one season I sat down and made a list. It took a few drafts, but I came up with one I liked. I went to the print shop and made a couple dozen copies. Now when I pack for a hunt,

I pull out the list and start packing. And I don't forget anything.

Ron Eamon
Blodgett, Oregon

This is a master list of "stuff" we take hunting when it is possible to drive to our campsite. It fills an enclosed four-by-eight-foot or five-by-eight-foot U-Haul trailer, with room left for 2 cut-up elk carcasses as well. Many would say it is too much stuff, but if you need it, you need it. Obviously, some items are to simply make the trip as comfortable and enjoyable as possible.

Tow rope or chain
Mechanics tool kit
Tire chains and fasteners
High lift jack
Board for high lift jack base
Jumper cables
Tire pump
Tire chains
Axe
Shovel
Reflectors

Padlock with keys for trailer
Duct tape
3-in-1 oil

Plastic bucket
Lawn chairs
Sleeping tent
Cook tent
Tent poles
Tarps for tents
Extra tarps
Grommet kit
Rope
Foam mattress
Air mattress
Tent broom
Sleeping bags
Down bags
Pillows
Blankets

Tent heater
1 gallon kerosene or
  diesel (for firestarter)
Lantern fuel
Funnel
Extra mantels
Grill and legs
Wood stove
Propane stove
Propane tank and hose
Toilet seat
2x4s for toilet frame
Tarp poles
Double-headed nails

Waterless hand cleaner
Outdoor carpet for tent
  entry
Stove wire
Rake
Hammer
Nails
Spikes
10-foot 2x4
10-foot 2x2
6-foot 1x10
Chain saw
Saw fuel
Bar oil
Saw tool
Chain file
Hot water barrel

Dutch oven
Frying pans
Cooking pots
Big spoons
Spatulas
Tongs
Potato peeler
Can opener
Butcher knife
Coffee pot
Cutting board
Plastic wash basin
Dish soap
Towels
Plates, bowls, cups
Glasses
Eating utensils
Aluminum foil
Trash bags
Plastic water jugs
Baggies
Toilet paper
Paper towels
Paper plates
Ice
Ice chests
Large freighter pack
Daypack

Rifles
Spare rifle
Ammunition

Gun cases
Ammo pouch
Gun cleaning kit
Elk calls
Pocket knife
Hunting knives
Knife sharpeners
Meat saw (camp)
Meat saw (pack)
Come-along
Game hoist
Parachute cord
Fluorescent tape
Game bags
Liver bag
Camera and film
VCR camera
VCR film
VCR batteries
Battery charger
Binoculars
Tripod
Spotting scope
Aerial photos
Hand lens
Quadrangle maps
USFS maps
Suspenders
Belt
Wallet
License
Leather boots

Mickey Mouse boots
Camp boots
Down coat
Down vest
Billed hat
Stocking cap
Wool pants
Cotton pants
Socks

Shirts
Underwear
Thermal underwear
Thermal-wick socks
Poncho
Parka
Orange gloves
Wool gloves
Down gloves
Leather gloves
Face mask
Watch
Lighter
Eyeglasses
First-aid kit
Matches
String
Large flashlight and
    batteries
Small flashlight and
    batteries
Watch

Compass

Canteen

Special medicines

Aspirin and Tylenol

Toothbrush and toothpaste

Shaving gear

Soap

Hankies

Clean-wipes

Baby powder

Chapstick

Cortisone cream (bung
medicine)

Bag balm (ditto)

Kleenex

Sunglasses

Sunscreen

Lotion

Pistol and ammo

Radio and batteries

Skoal

Scotch

Soda

Money

Lt. Col. Mark R. Welch
Albuquerque, New Mexico

Here's a way to quickly count points on a bull elk:
The tallest point pointing straight up on a bull's
rack, while his head is straight out is the number
four point; just start at this number four point and
add whatever he has behind it and you will know
how many points he has total. One more makes him
a 5x5 and an easily spotted fork behind this long
number four tine makes him a 6x6 and so on. Even
at great distances this method works great. I teach
this little trick to all my elk hunters as I have a "four
point minimum" rule on my hunting land.

Al Marohn
Pickett, Wisconsin

Bulls won't grow to be six-pointers if you shoot them when they are young. If you really are a trophy hunter, let those young bulls grow for another year or two and instead crop an old cow for the freezer. Trophy bulls are produced by healthy elk herds; help get those bull/cow ratios where they should be. Make a personal rule that you will never shoot a bull for its antlers unless it is bigger than any you have already shot.

Tory Taylor
Dubois, Wyoming

Don't go into the woods with the idea that you "have" to kill something. Be alert to your surroundings. Take joy in the bird that lands on a limb right next to you or the "ratchet-jawed" squirrel that has just sounded the alert. God has put all of these things there for our enjoyment, so make the most of it. When you come back to camp at night empty handed you won't be disappointed because you will have memories of the day that go beyond the killing.

Jeff Keller
Bend, Oregon

Leave the woods cleaner than you found it. Don't spoil the beauty with litter and cigarette butts.

If on a road you are unfamiliar with, pull over at a wide spot to check your map. Roadway courtesy will go a long way with those who are behind you and would like to get around.

Encourage fellow hunters to be polite and ethical. Keep a good attitude. There may be some low times, especially if you have built this up to be the "hunt of a lifetime." Remember, there is more to the hunt than getting game. You can remember yourself as an encourager or a "Gloomy Gus." Attitude makes the difference. One guy can spoil a good time or one guy can make this hunt a great hunt.

If you come upon a person who needs help with downed game, help them. After the game is located, compliment them on the fine animal they have taken. Nobody wants their "moment in the sun" shattered by someone's jealousy or rudeness. The same thing applies to another's rifle. Don't joke or poke fun.

Treat others and the property of others as you would want to be treated and as you would want your property to be treated.

Butch Grusing
Fountain, Colorado

I have a saying: You need to pick your hunting partner with as much care as you pick your spouse. I have found that a good partner has to be as driven as you in your desire to put out the effort to enjoy the hunt. If you go with someone who is a 5 in desire and you are a 9, you are not going to have a good time. Also when he is depressed you need to be up, and vice versa. My partner and I have been together 6 years now and we always have a great hunt no matter what is hanging on the meat pole.

Keep a diary of your hunt. Every evening after dinner we write down where we went, what we saw, and we keep a running total of elk seen, both cows and bulls, and we keep track of "close encounters" which are times when we were within 50 yards or so of elk and they were unaware of us. We really enjoy going over these notes after the hunt and we realize just how much fun we had.

Sally Bayliss
Roseburg, Oregon

As truly one of the greatest elk hunters who has ever lived, I have found the secret of a successful hunt. First, understand that I spend more time hunting than others. I haven't wasted time tracking wounded elk, cleaning a bull, or hauling elk off the mountain. I spend all my time hunting elk. I have hunted elk all over the West. I have packed horseback into wilderness areas to find no snow or too much snow. I've hunted private ranches and public land. I have hunted one of the big ranches you see on the television hunting shows. I've hunted with famous outdoor writers and big time booking agents. Still, I have never killed a bull elk.

Through all of this, I have learned the secret: Enjoy every moment. Savor the sunrises and sunsets.

Listen to the sounds and take a nap in the warm afternoon sun. Learn your horses name, pick up a tip or two from your guide, and watch all types of wildlife, not just the species you are hunting. The joy of hunting is: The hunting. If you fill your tag you've gotten a bonus.

J. Jay Hill
Salt Lake City, Utah

Rocky Mountain
<u>Elk Foundation</u>

Elk country. It's crystal, snow-fed streams and golden, sun-touched valleys. It's mountain meadows studded with multicolored wildflowers and mysterious dark stands of lodgepole. And it's threatened. The stunning landscapes that fill North America's elk country attract not only a diversity of wildlife, but also increasing numbers of people. And, as people move in, wildlife must move out.

While development chips away at critical wildlife ranges, the Rocky Mountain Elk Foundation works to ensure that elk and other wildlife aren't left without a home. Since its inception in 1984, the Elk Foundation has completed 4,700 conservation projects in 48 states and eight provinces, conserving and enhancing more than 4.5 million acres of wildlife habitat (as of January 2006).

Join Us!

Faced with increasing obstacles, wildlife conservation demands a spirited team effort. Thanks to thousands of enthusiastic RMEF members working together, North America's wildlife enjoys a more secure future. When you sign up as an RMEF member, you join a group of dedicated folks leaving a lasting wildlife legacy.

As a **Supporting Member**, you'll receive:
- 6 issues of *Bugle* magazine •
- Personalized membership card •
- Elk Foundation decal •
- Gift catalogs •

For more information about the Rocky Mountain Elk Foundation and how you can become involved, please call **1-800-CALL ELK (225-5355).**

• • • • • • • • •

*The mission of the Rocky Mountain Elk Foundation is
to ensure the future of elk, other wildlife and their habitat.*

Rocky Mountain Elk Foundation
5705 Grant Creek Road
Missoula, Montana 59808